" As compressed within the bounded shell
Boundless Ocean seems to surge and swell,
Haunting echoes of an infinite whole
Moan and murmur through Man's finite soul."–
MATHILDE BLIND.

" In a symbol there is concealment and yet revelation,
silence and speech acting together, some embodiment
and revelation of the infinite, made to blend itself with
the finite, to stand visible and, as it were, attainable
there."—THOMAS CARLYLE.

" Then knew I that he had given me the symbols of
the four quarters of the earth, and of all the worlds of
the universe ; the stone for the North, the sword for
the East, the spear for the South, and the cup for the
West."—FIONA MACLEOD.

" Our spirits have climbed high,—
*   *   *   *   *
And from the top of sense, looked over sense
To the significance and heart of things
Rather than things themselves."–
ELIZABETH B. BROWNING.

Symbolism
of the East and West

By

Mrs Murray-Aynsley

With Introduction by

Sir George C. M. Birdwood, M.D., K.C.I.E., C.S.I., LL.D.

With Plates and other Illustrations

KENNIKAT PRESS
Port Washington, N. Y./London

SYMBOLISM OF THE EAST AND WEST

First published in 1900
Reissued in 1971 by Kennikat Press
Library of Congress Catalog Card No: 74-118538
ISBN 0-8046-1162-9

Manufactured by Taylor Publishing Company   Dallas, Texas

PREFACE

My knowledge of India began twenty-one years ago, and almost the half of this interval has been spent in wanderings over that vast continent, from Cape Comorin in the South, to Peshawar on our Northern frontier; a large portion of the remainder has been occupied in European travel, during which I always sought for, and noted in museums and elsewhere, any objects or customs bearing upon Eastern Symbolism. Since their original appearance in the *Indian Antiquary* much has been added to these papers relative to Folk-Lore and Folk-Customs in Europe.

One of the results of the present increased facilities of locomotion has been a growth of new ideas in various countries, and especially in some hitherto isolated districts; thereby many curious old customs and superstitions (of much assistance to us in tracing the connection between East and West) are doomed to speedy extinction. No time is to be lost, then, by travellers who would witness and record their existence. It would seem, therefore, most desirable to stimulate research in this direction, and by the publication of a work like the present, to enable the individual traveller to recognise any ancient customs or symbols he may meet with.

In the following pages I have to some extent brought together the results of laborious researches made by various students, but I hope also that some of the ideas and features of my work will be found to be new ones. Their chief object is to furnish a collection of facts, bearing upon customs and symbols in particular, gathered during many journeys in various lands, and of Folk-Lore in general, as shown in many superstitions still abiding, even in England ; and I propose also to illustrate this work with drawings of the different symbols, to assist those who may not be able to wander as far as I have done to prosecute further researches into the most interesting, but to a great extent, unsolved problem of the origin of certain peoples and races in Europe and elsewhere.

HARRIET G. M. MURRAY-AYNSLEY.

SRINAGAR, KASHMIR,
September 1896.

CONTENTS

CHAPTER I

INTRODUCTORY

CHAPTER II

SUN WORSHIP

CHAPTER III

SUN AND CUP AND MOON SYMBOLS

Contents

Contents

CHAPTER VII

SOME IDEAS ABOUT THE FUTURE LIFE

CHAPTER VIII

SACRED TREES

CHAPTER IX

SNAKE WORSHIP

CHAPTER X

THE EVIL EYE AND ALLIED NOTIONS

Contents

LIST OF PLATES

INTRODUCTION

THIS work, reproduced by its authoress, the late Mrs Murray-Aynsley, from the well-known articles originally contributed by her to the *Indian Antiquary*, is of special value to all scientific students of iconosemic Symbolism, consisting as it chiefly does, of a most interesting record of independent personal researches, carried on during twenty years of travel, in various and far-distant countries, by a writer singularly well qualified by natural ability, and her traditionary culture, to observe with intelligence, and in the spirit of truth and soberness. Her father was the Rev. Frederick Manners Sutton, of Kelham Hall, near Newark-on-Trent, a nephew of Charles Manners Sutton, Archbishop of Canterbury, father of the first Viscount Canterbury, and of Thomas Manners Sutton, Lord Chancellor of Ireland and first Baron Manners ; the two brothers being grandsons of John, eleventh Earl and third Duke of Rutland. Her mother was the Lady Henrietta Barbara Lumley, daughter of Richard, seventh Earl of Scarborough, Prebendary of York. Mrs Murray-Aynsley thus inherited, on both the maternal and the paternal side, all the potentiality of the thoroughly serviceable and trustworthy intellectual and moral qualities she possessed in such felicitous and prolific combination ; and I would add, for those who

know her only from her writings, that distinction of appearance, demeanour, and address, as of a portrait of Queen
Elizabeth stepping forth from its spacious frame, and of high-
bred womanly courtesy of manñer, which were the most im-
pressive outward and visible characteristics of her command-
ing and most gracious personality.   She had a remarkable
talent for languages, which greatly assisted her in communi-
cating directly with the peasantry in foreign countries; and
she had so thorough and scholarly a knowledge of French,
German, and Italian, that she both wrote and spoke in these
languages with, apparently, as complete ease as in English.
She early displayed a great delight in popular archæology,
customs, superstitions, and traditionary lore; and when at
Rome, where she constantly lived between 1850 and 1860,
she devoted herself to a systematic study of the architectural,
literary, social, and religious antiquities of the Eternal City.
She also had a great taste for certain picturesque branches of
natural history, such as mineralogy, botany, and conchology,
and while travelling in Algeria had the good fortune to discover one or two new species of sea shells, of which specimens
are now to be seen in the British Museum.

In 1875 Mr and Mrs Murray-Aynsley went out to India,
where, at intervals, down to 1897, they travelled for altogether
ten years, so absorbing was her interest in the country and
its people, and their religion and religious arts.   She was
especially fascinated by the analogies she observed between
the habits and usages of the antique people of modern India,
India of the Hindoos, and those of the allied pagan people of
ancient Rome and Greece.

During her frequent and prolonged tours through the

continent of India Mrs Murray-Aynsley collected her unique, and practically exhaustive, and inexhaustible store of information regarding the *svastika* of the Buddhists, Hindoos, and Mussulmans ; not compiling it from books on the Symbolism of Antiquity and the East, but collecting it, at first hand, from the people of the country themselves. Even her own writings on the subject give one no idea of the wonderful extent and thoroughness of her knowledge of the universal use of this symbol. For her first article on it she received the medal of the Masonic Society of the " Quatuor Coronati," and was made an Associate of the Order of Freemasons.

Early in 1896, at my suggestion, she undertook the preparation of the present volume ; and it is a matter of deep regret to me that, owing to delays, caused by my own ill-health, and other disabling preoccupations, she did not live to see its publication. Throughout the summer of 1898 she was engaged in writing a paper on the Folk Lore of Guernsey for the meeting of the British Association to be held at Bristol in the autumn of that year. But she never recovered her strength after an attack of influenza from which she suffered greatly in the winter of 1897-98 ; and having caught a chill at a garden party at the end of last July, pneumonia set in after a few days, and she died on the 6th of August following, in the 72nd year of her age ; dying, as she had continuously lived for over half a century, a true-hearted and high-minded priestess of the past, with all her thoughts diligently directed to the humanising study of her chosen departments of historical research.

One of the most instructive chapters in Mrs Murray-Aynsley's book is the fourth, on the *svastika*, a sun symbol

of the hoariest antiquity, and still equally reverenced throughout the East by Buddhists, and Hindoos, and Mahometans,
as a talisman of the highest auspiciousness and potency. This
symbol had attracted the attention of European antiquarians
long before they began to recognise it as a symbol of the
revolving sun. The late Edward Thomas, the most accomplished oriental numismatist of our generation, was the first to
point out, in Vol. XX. [1880] of the *Numismatic Chronicle,*
that in certain ancient coins the Solar Wheel was replaced by
the *svastika.* It was obvious that the *svastika* on these coins
was an abbreviated Solar Wheel, with four spokes instead of
twelve, the tyre, and the direction of the revolution of the
wheel, being indicated by the crossbars (or crampions) of the
svastika. But the decisive proof of the fact was the discovery
made by Percy Gardner, and announced in the same volume
of the *Numismatic Chronicle* [see also the *Athenæum* of
13th August 1892], that the name of the Thracian town of
Mesembria [the Megarean, not the Samothracian Mesembria],
meaning " the (city of the) Mid-day (sun) " is figured on some
of its coins by the syllable Mes, followed by the *svastika,*
as the equivalent of *embria,* that is *hemeria.*

There is another interesting proof of the *svastika* being a
symbol of revolving movement, if not of solar revolution, to
be found in Mr Alfred T. Butler's work on *The Ancient
Coptic Churches.* In Vol. I., ch. iii., Mr Butler describes the
church of *Abu-'s Sefain,* "Father of the Two-Swords," dating
from the 10th century. In the open court behind the *man-
darah,* or Reception Room, is an enclosed flour mill, the big
cog-wheel of which revolves on a heavy pivot, turning,
above, in a solid beam, on which are deeply carved, side by

side, a triangle, symbolising the Christian Trinity, and the
svastika, here possibly signifying that all things living, "live,
and move, and have their being" in God. Indeed the
highest symbolism of the *svastika* might well be expressed in Goethe's words : God's is the East, God's is
the West, North and South lands repose in peace in His
Hände :—

> "Gottes ist der Orient !
> Gottes ist der Occident !
> Nord- und südliches Gelände
> Ruht im Frieden seiner Hände." *

There may be no connection between the Assyro-Baby-
lonian name for the sun, *Samas*, in Hebrew *Shemesh*, and
the Greek *semeion*, "a mask," "a device," "a sign," "a con-
stellation," "a token." But the earliest Akkadian name of
the sun, *Kasseba* [*cf.* Cassiopea], is rendered in Assyro-Baby-
lonian by *tsalam* [*cf.* the Sun-goddess Salambo] meaning
"image," "symbol." This is the Arabic *tilsam*, in the plural
talasim, from which comes, through the Spanish, our "talisman," and possibly the Greek *telesma*, "a payment," "initiation," "mystery." The sun, so magnificently apostrophised
by Satan, in *Paradise Lost*, B. IV. 31-7 :—

> "O thou, that, with surpassing glory crowned,
> Look'st from thy sole dominion like the God
> Of this new world ; at whose sight all the stars
> Hide their diminished heads, to thee I call,
> O Sun !"

---

* *Cf.* Aratus, *Phænomena*, 1-5 [quoted in "The Acts of the Apostles," xvii.
28-29] :—"Let us begin with Zeus ; let us always call upon, and laud his name ; all
the network of interwending roads and all the busy markets of mankind are full of
Zeus, and all the paths and fair havens of the seas ; and everywhere our hope is
in Zeus, for we are also his children." *Cf.* also the quotation, facing the Title
Page, from Fiona Macleod, *Dominion of Dreams*, "The Book of the Opal."

—"The Ancient of Days" of Dan. vii. 9, 13, and 22 ;—"the Sun of Righteousness . . . with healing in his wings" of Malachi iv. 2 ;—"the worshipp'd Sun," is thus revealed to us, in the oldest of its Old World names, as the first, as well as greatest, of talismans :* and its symbols, the Wheel, the *svastika*, and the "Equinoctial," or "Greek Cross," were probably the earliest figured by the human race, not excepting those ancestral, progenitory, and phallic symbols, with which the sun symbols are so often found combined.

* Similarly *phulake*, the Greek for "caution," "watching," "being on one's guard," was the original phylactery, "serving as a safeguard," and prophylactic, "advanced guard," "outpost," &c. The original symbol [from the Greek *sumballein*, "to throw together," "bring together," "compare," "contract," "covenant," etc.] was a "pledge" to pay one's proportion of the cost of a Greek drinking match ; and hence a "passport" to such a carouse ; and any "passport" ; and the actual contribution toward the bill ; and the debauch itself ; and, finally, any common meal. It is partly in the last sense that the term symbol is sometimes applied to the elements of the sacrament of the Eucharist. The pledge might be one's clothes,—literally a "pawn"; but usually it was the signet-ring, or the impression, that is, the signature, of it, on clay or wax ; and hence a symbol came to mean any credential of authenticity and claim. This may also partly explain the application of the term to a "creed,"—as a "passport" to heaven,—as in the instance of the "Symbolum Apostolicum"; although Rufinus applies the term thereto in translation of "collatio,"—"id quod plures in unum conferunt" ; and the use of the latter term in the connection is the source of the notion that each of the Apostles contributed an article to the Creed called after them. A symbol as an impressed signature is a significant image ; and as soon as this was recognised it was at once used all over Anterior Asia, and Egypt, and throughout southern Europe as an outward and visible sign of mental ideas, and particularly of religious ideas. The practice indeed became universal of conveying sacerdotal dogmas and doctrines by means of iconosemic symbols, including all kinds of ideographic representation ; and their immemorial appropriation to religious subjects has always given these glyptic, plastic, fictile, and painted symbols a character of sanctity unknown to any other kind of hierography. With its enlarged divine significance the symbol became identified with the oracle, the omen, and the talisman, defensive and offensive. The amulet [Arabic, *hama'il*, "borne," *tawiz*, "a refuge," *hijab*, "a cover," *cf.* the Hindustani *hamal*, "a porter," "a bearer," in the sense of *Henry and his Bearer*, and the Greek *periamma* and *periapton*] was 'originally a talisman, or talismanic symbol, worn about the body, usually round the neck ; but the term has always included any talisman, at least from the time of the Romans, who named the

Mrs Murray-Aynsley's eighth chapter on "Sacred Trees" is also of great, because of still living, and wide-spread interest. The tree has from the most primitive periods played a part in the religion of all the races of mankind, as a striking symbol of life, concrete and abstract, individual and universal; and as, moreover, in itself, a manifest divinity. No religious symbol has impressed itself so ubiquitously, so demonstratively, and so indissolubly, on the decorative arts of the civilised world; and far enlightening are the surprises in the path of those who turn to trace it through its infinite artistic permutations in Greece, and Rome, and under the Saracens, and in modern Europe, back to its original hieratic forms in Egypt and Mesopotamia. Even the worship of the tree still survives throughout Christendom in a variety of popular customs, prehistorically established in celebration of the annual revival of vegetation between the Spring Equinox [25th March—Our Lady Day] and the Summer Solstice [24th June—St John's Day]. Among them are dancing round the Maypole, and the May mummery of "Jack in the Green," once generally observed in this country on the 1st of May; the festival of "Green George," or "St George in the Green," held in Carinthia on St George's Day, [23rd April]; the Whitsuntide floral festivities of

Cyclamen hederæfolium, "Amuletum," because, as they thought, [Pliny xxv. 9 (67)] :—"Wherever it grows harmful spells have no effect." Symbola, in Arcadia, was so called, because it marked the confluence ["meetings"] of a number of small springs with the Alpheus, close by its source at Phylace [cf. Sanskrit, sangama, and Sungum, in the delta of the Ganges]. Balaklava was in ancient times called Symbolon Portus, either because it was a "Semaphore Station," or because it was united, as a defence against the Scyths, to Chersonesus [Sevastopol] and Eupatorium [Inkerman] by a wall [cf. Sanskrit sanga, "a bridge"]; or, possibly, because it was a "Treaty Port"; but why Symbolum, in Thrace, was so called, I do not know.

Holland; and the festival of St John, held in Sweden on the eve [23rd June] of St John's Day, when young fir trees are set up before every house, and arbours are everywhere constructed of fir-branches, and the people sit out in them, eating and drinking, and merry-making, all the night through.

In the New World of America, especially among the Protestant Anglo-Saxons of North America, the historical tradition of the divinity of the tree would naturally be weak; yet so strong is the feeling of actual consanguinity and fellowship, and of worship, with which all men, and emphatically the Aryan races, regard the tree, that the people of the United States, a few years ago, established a new vernal festival under the name of Arbor Day. This beneficent festival is a moveable feast, the date of its celebration varying, according to the climatic conditions of different parts of the States, from the 1st of April to the 31st of May. It was first held in Nebraska, on a Resolution of the Board of Agriculture moved by Mr J. Sterling Morton, setting apart the 10th of April 1872, as "Tree-planting Day." In April 1874, the second Wednesday of April was proclaimed as "Arbor Day," and in 1885, the 22nd of April was permanently fixed as Arbor Day for Nebraska. In 1876, Michigan and Minnesota followed the example of Nebraska, and, finally, New York in 1888; in which year, on the 30th of April, an act was passed decreeing that "the Friday following the 1st of May in each year shall hereafter be known throughout this State as Arbor Day." By a popular vote of the State Schools the "White Elm" was declared to be the "Tree of the State," and the Rose of Spring, in all its grace of budding beauty, the "Queen of Flowers." Perhaps they were thinking of the

monumental brass formerly in Westminster Abbey, bearing
a crowned rose, with the legend round it :—

> " Sis Rosa, flos florum
> Morbis medicina meorum."

The United States were at once imitated by the Dominion
of Canada ; and in 1896, by Spain, where King Alphonso
XIII. fixed the 26th of March for the annual celebration of
the *Fiesta del Arbol*. Attempts have been made to establish
Arbor Day in this country, but they have been but sporadic,
local, and altogether casual efforts, made chiefly in connection
with the movement initiated by Mr Radcliffe Cooke, for
the improvement of the apple orchards in the cyder-making
counties of the United Kingdom.   The oak was the indigenous
" Sacred Tree " of the Druids ; but the apple was, undoubtedly,
one of the Sacred Trees which the first Aryan immigrants
brought with themselves from the continent into the British
Isles ; and, considering the natural importance of the revival
of cyder-making in the West of England and the South of
Ireland, it is greatly to be desired that an Arbor Day should
be founded in this country by Act of Parliament, for the
express purpose of replanting our worn-out apple orchards, and
extending the cultivation of fruit trees generally, throughout
the United Kingdom.   If this is ever done, our Arbor Day
should be fixed on the 1st of November, or old " Apple
Fruit Day," now All Saints' Day, the Christian substitute for
the Roman festival of Pomona, and, in these islands, also, of
the first day of the Celtic Feast of Saman [Shaman, Shony],
the Lord of Death.   It follows All Hallow Even, or Halloween,
the Christian substitute for the Vigil of Saman, and precedes
All Souls' Day, the Christian substitute of the second day of

the Druidical Feast of Saman.   Following the ingathering of
the summer harvests, and preceding the long night of winter,
it was a season of great rejoicings, accompanied always by the
drinking of what we in after times came to call Lambs-wool.
This is generally explained as some drink,—ale, or cyder,
or mead, or milk,—with toasted apples thrown into it, the
appearance of these apples, as of tufts of lambs' wool, giving
as is said, its name to the drink.   But Charles Vallancy, the
antiquary, says :—" The first day of November was dedicated
to the angel [*i.e.* resuscitated Pomona] presiding over fruits,
and seeds, and was therefore named La Mas Ubhal, that is the
day of the apple fruit, and being pronounced Lamasool, the
English have corrupted the name to Lambs-wool."

It was the apple tree of the pre-historic Celtic immigrants
that gave to the whole peninsula of " the West of England"
[Gloucestershire, Somersetshire, Dorsetshire, Devonshire,
and Cornwall], stretching vaguely from roving Camelot to
Lyonesse,

"The wave-worn kingdom of Romance,"

the name of "ancient Avalon" [Avelion, "Avaloniæ insula,"
" Apple Island "] :—

" Deep meadowed, happy, fair with orchard lawns
And bowery hollows, crowned with summer seas." *

Mrs Murray-Aynsley's chapters on " Sun Worship and its

* It is well to beware of restricting the location in actual geography of by-gone
places, the names of which have passed into remote romance, and myth, and
faery.   Camelot has been identified with Winchester, with Queen's Camel, and
with Camelford.   But *camel* in Camelot is formed from the Celtic word *cam*,
"crooked," "bent," "bowed," "bayed," as in Cambus [*camus*], Cambuskenneth,
Cambridge [the Cambridgeshire not the Gloucestershire Cambridge, the name of
the latter town being corrupted from Cwatbridge, " the Bridge of Omens "], More-
cambe Bay, etc., and again in the clan-name Campbell : whereas in Queen's Camel

Symbols, including the *svastika*," on "Sacred Stones," on "Snake Worship," and the others on "the Evil Eye," "the Future Life," " the Wild Huntsman of Northern Europe, and his possible Asiatic Origin," on " Architectural Customs," and on " Spain and Further Europe," are all full of new facts and suggestions in elucidation of the obscure and fascinating subjects of which they treat. A systematic student might regret, that before recasting the notes of her original observations into

and Camelford it is a form of the Anglo-Saxon *gafol*, *cf.* ["guild"] " tribute," as in Guildford [Astolat]. In England, Camelot may be centred in Somersetshire, Avalon in Devonshire, and Lyonesse, of which the asphodel [daffodil] wreathed Scilly islands are the submerged peaks, in Cornwall. They are however also cloud-lands of the setting sun, "the Sacred West," the aboriginal, Phœnician, Europe, and have no definite boundaries, at least, not on their heavenward marches. As for Avalon, which has been restricted to Glastonbury, we find an Avella Vecchia, the Latin Abella, in Italy ; an Avallon, in the Department of the Yonne, in France ; and that Emhaim Ablach, "the island of the Apple Tree" was the old Gaelic name of the island of Arran [*i.e.* Aran " Ploughed," *cf.* Arrochar, and the Latin "aratum," also Arthur, and its equivalent George, both these personal names having also reference to the sun as the heavenly Husbandman, or Ploughman]. Morien [Owen Morgan], in his *Light of Britain*, p. 78, where he translates Ynys Avalon, as "the Island of the Everlasting Apple," says the phrase refers to the whole of Britain, as the Sacred Island of the Sun, the golden apple of the eternal heavens. The Anglo-Saxon, and the Norse distribution of the apple tree, as distinguished from the Celtic distribution, is marked in England by such place names as Appleby, Appledore, and Applethorpe, and Appuldercomb, and Maple Durham [*i.e.* Mapuldur—ham]. All these Celtic, Anglo-Saxon, and Norse place names have been ingeniously surmised to be corrupted from the name of the aforesaid Campanian town of Abella ; and the line in Virgil's Æneid, vii. 740, has been cited :—"Et quos maliferae despectant mœnia Abellæ," to prove that it was a great centre of apple planting. Abella obviously derived its name from a common source with *abhal, ubhal, obulas, apfel*, and " apple " ; but was famous for its filberts, " nuces Avellane," the "Avelines" of the French, and not for apples ; and "malifera," in the above quoted line simply means, "fruit-bearing," the specific Latin designation of the apple being "pomum." Thomas Fuller, referring to the apple-growing, cyder-making, country of Hereford, observed that it is more worthy than the well-known Prussian province of the denomination of Pomerania [Pommern] ; but this last place name is the Latinised form of the Sclavonic *po* "by," or " on," and *marya*, "the sea," and is the equivalent of Super Mare, and Marina. Why the principal island of the Orkneys is called Pomona, I do not know.

the form and dignity of a book, she had not collated them with such standard works of recent production as Count Goblet D'Alviella's *Migrations of Symbols,* and Frazer's *Golden Bough.* But probably it is well that she did´ not. The comprehensive generalisations of these remarkable publications might have distracted, and even biased, her own keen and close natural powers of observation, and would certainly have affected the spontaneous and independent manner in which her personal observations were carried out, and are here placed on permanent record. As already stated, the empirical, idiomatic method of the enquiries she pursued, not only constitutes their characteristic charm for the general reader, but their specific value for the specialist in Symbolism; and the pre-eminent merit of Mrs Murray-Aynsley's volume, representing as it does the steadfast, fruitful labours of a lifetime, is that it can be recommended with equal confidence to them both. May various Fate once more approve of it the truth of the proverbial text :—

" Dii laboribus omnia vendunt."

GEORGE BIRDWOOD.

24th June 1899.

CHAPTER I

WHEN we find the same customs, arts, and practices existing amongst peoples living on widely separated continents, we may reasonably conclude that either such practices and customs have had a common origin, or that—if they are not such as would naturally suggest themselves to primitive races—the peoples themselves are derived from a common aboriginal stock.

The arts and customs of the so-called Stone Age of Scandinavia, of the present natives of New Zealand, and of certain parts of Africa, while they present resemblances, belong to races of distinct stocks, whose development in arts and manufactures never enabled them to do more than supply the absolute needs of their existence ; but, as regards the more civilised races of Central Asia and Europe, it seems very possible that their manners and customs have proceeded from a common source.

The date of the commencement of the Stone Age is, of course, conjectural. It has been put at from 3000 to 5000 years ago. The race which lived in it is now probably represented in Europe by the Finns, the Lapps, and the Eskimo, because implements have been in use almost down to our own times in the countries inhabited by the two latter peoples which are very similar in form to those that have been discovered in graves and bogs in Scandinavia and classed as belonging to the Stone Age. The peoples who used stone implements in the North of Europe, and were ignorant of the use of metals, belonged to what·is styled the *non*-Aryan races; they were probably stone worshippers also. It would seem highly probable, therefore, that aboriginal races existed contemporaneously both in Asia and in Europe,—for it is hardly credible that, with such appliances as the people of the Stone Age possessed, they could have wandered from one continent to the other, and (supposing them to have come from the same stock as the Śaiva worshippers of Asia) have made their way to Scandinavia through Siberia and Russia, cutting a path through the dense forests which are supposed to have then existed in those regions. Non-Aryan stone worship is very possibly nearly, if not quite, as ancient as the Aryan worship of the Sun, the Planets, and of Fire. To this day, both in Asia and in Europe, the *non*-Aryan races appear to be those who seem capable of, and who have consequently attained to, only the lowest type of civilisation. They differ essentially from the Aryans in type and in features: those of India seem to be wanting both in self-respect and in natural intelligence.

Judging from the remains of prehistoric art in the Museums of Denmark, Norway, and Sweden, it would seem as if two great waves of Aryan peoples (conquerors of non-Aryans) had made their way from Central Asia into Scandinavia at different and widely separated intervals. The advent of the first of these—the workers in bronze—has been placed about 1000 B.C.; they are believed to have belonged to what we style the Keltic race. They may have come from the Highlands of Central Asia by a northern route, passing through Siberia and Russia,—for in this latter country ornaments have been found similar in character to those which have been discovered in graves in Scandinavia and classed as belonging to the Bronze Age. Those who have examined the designs on the ornaments of gold and silver now worn by the natives of Asia will, we think, have no difficulty in tracing the resemblance which many of the patterns and forms of the Scandinavian finds bear to them. It seems very possible that these workers in bronze, on their arrival in Scandinavia, found it already, at least partially, occupied by the non-Aryans of the Stone Age, who retired or disappeared before them. In like manner, we imagine, the workers of the Bronze Age may, in their turn, have been dispossessed in Scandinavia by a second Aryan race, who introduced weapons of iron. The country naturally remained in the possession of the strongest : in the hands of those who were provided with the best weapons and had attained the highest degree of civilisation. The people of the Bronze Age were acquainted with gold ; some of their goldsmiths' work, both in design and in execution, surpasses anything we now produce. This may seem a bold assertion, but we think it will be borne out by a reference to specimens in the museums of Copenhagen and Stockholm.

Gold was largely used in Scandinavia in the manufacture of articles for personal adornment, of cups for sacrificial or funeral purposes, and also for barter. Coils of gold, about the thickness of an ordinary cedar pencil, have been found there : and it has been conjectured from their appearance that these were carried on the person, and pieces cut off

as required.   Silver does not appear in Scandinavia until the
Iron Age, when it was used for bracelets, brooches, chains, etc.
We must not, however, fall into the error of imagining that
these three periods of stone, bronze, and iron were con-
temporaneous in the various countries of Europe.   Thus
Scandinavia did not receive Christianity till the eleventh
century, and it may also have been far behindhand in
emerging from its primitive customs.   Again, the bronze
and the iron ages would there appear to have overlapped
each other, for implements and weapons of both bronze and
iron have been found together in these Northern lands.
Judging from the specimens in various museums, articles or
fragments of bronze have never been found in Scandinavia
in connection with stone celts, whereas, in some of the
dolmens or tombs of the prehistoric people who inhabited
Brittany, stone implements and pieces of bronze have been
found side by side, and pieces of the same metal have also
been discovered amongst the deposits of human ashes which
have not unfrequently been laid bare on excavating round
the bases of the *Menhirs* or huge unhewn slabs of stone
which the aboriginal inhabitants of that province placed
upright in great numbers.   A bronze bracelet was also
found some years ago in the island of Guernsey on excavating the dolmen called Dehus.   It is the opinion of some
archæologists that in this case, as also in Brittany, there had
been a second and later interment in the same grave, the
first during the Stone Age and the second in the Keltic or
Bronze Age.

In Brittany, too, the Iron Age was distinct from the
Bronze Age.   The people of the Iron Age in Sweden and

Norway are best known to us under the name of the Goths, who are thought to have appeared in these countries about the year 100 A.D. They may have been a portion of a second wave of immigration from Eastern lands; they belong to the last stages of prehistoric times. According to Ferishtah, the Persian historian, the *bearded* races represented the Aryans, who early settled in India, and probably occupied it when the Greeks knew it best. The *beardless* people, on the other hand, may be held to represent the less pure races who occupied the whole of the valley of the Ganges, and were practically the people who were converted by Buddha to his new form of faith.

At this distance of time it would at first sight appear incredible that the *non*-Aryan peoples of Northern Europe should have any resemblance in type or features to *non*-Aryans in Asia. From personal experience I can quote one instance in which this would seem to be the case—viz., between the Eskimo and the inhabitants of the Spiti valley, a remote district in the Himâlayas. In spite of its apparent improbability, what renders it possible that this resemblance is not an accidental one is that the Eskimo and this Asiatic race would appear to have remained almost if not absolutely pure, owing to their natural surroundings being such as to isolate them from the rest of the world.

The Spiti valley is from 130 to 150 miles in length: it connects the extreme upper part of the Satlaj valley with the Lahûl valley. At its eastern end it is entered by the Hangrang Pass—over 14,000 feet above sea level, and at the other extremity the Bara Lâchâ, 16,000 feet, must be crossed in order to enter Lahaul: consequently,

during many months in the year, no one can enter or leave
Spiti. As might be expected, its inhabitants are a rude,
hardy race of mountaineers, their language is a dialect of
Tibetan, their religion, Buddhism. In the autumn of 1881
we spent about four weeks in that valley, and thus had
ample opportunities of observing the people, since occasionally upwards of fifty natives of both sexes accompanied
us as coolies on our marches, and our arrival in a village
was a signal for the whole population to turn out—a
European face being as rare a sight to them as a white
crow. The British Assistant Commissioner of Kulu visits
this valley every second or third year only. Any crimes or
disputes which may occur amongst them in the interval are
referred to their hereditary native Governor, who is styled
" the Nono."

Almost without exception, the women of Spiti are very
short in stature and broad in proportion to their height,
but they are very muscular, as was evidenced by their
carrying heavy loads up the mountains, singing in chorus
the whole way. Though not as dark as the natives of
India, their complexion has a sallowish tint, tending to olive ;
they have straight dark hair, remarkably high cheek bones,
small and slightly oblique eyes.

The general contour of the face is extremely irregular,
the forehead broad, but flat. The women wear a sort of
pork-pie hat made of dark woollen cloth, their dress is a
coat of dark blue or brown cloth reaching down below the
knees, and confined at the waist with a rope or sash. On
their feet both sexes wear high boots or leggings, made,
like the rest of their attire, of home spun and home woven

wool; the foot has the additional protection of leather or partially dressed skins.

In 1883, when visiting the Ethnological Museum at Copenhagen, it was most curious and interesting to see in one of the glass cases a life-sized model, in wood or plaster, which professed to be an exact representation of the first Eskimo woman ever brought to Denmark—about sixty years previously. This figure bears a wonderful likeness in every respect to the type of the women of the Spiti valley, and it was impossible to help exclaiming, " That is a woman from Spiti, but she is dressed in skins instead of in cloth garments."

Supposing, too, any of the natives of Spiti to have wandered thus far, Greenland would be a climate which might suit them. When, on leaving Spiti, we reached Darcha in the Lahaul valley, though this place is at an altitude of 12,500 feet, our whole staff of coolies, whom we had hoped to take with us a couple of marches (days) more, bolted back to their own country at 3 A.M., saying it was so hot they could not bear it an hour longer.

Whilst we are on the subject of the great similarity in dress and appearance between people inhabiting different continents, it may not be out of place to remark that the above is not a solitary example as far as the dress is concerned. The whole attire of the women of the Kulu valley consists of a long woollen scarf or shawl of home manufacture, a portion of which forms the petticoat—held in position by a girdle—whilst the remainder is so arranged as to cover the whole bust, leaving the arms free. This garment is fastened on each side of the chest by a brass

brooch of the Runic form.   It is a curious fact, but surely
hardly an accidental circumstance, that in Africa the women
belonging to the Nomad tribes of the Sahara clothe themselves in precisely the same fashion, except that the one
garment of these latter is of calico, and the two brooches—
equally of the Runic or penannular form—are made of a
debased kind of silver.

Again, a kind of cloth, made of the natural brown and
white sheep's wool, is occasionally made at the present day
in Kashmir ; it has a geometric pattern woven into it.   The
natives there say that only a small quantity of it is made,
as it is troublesome to weave.   Curious to relate, fragments
of woollen material, with the same design woven in, have
been found in some ancient graves in Scandinavia, which are
supposed to date from the Bronze Age (Dr Hans Hildebrand's *Handbook of Scandinavian Arts*).   An exactly similar
material is still woven by the peasants on the File Fjeld in
Norway for their own use only : the design is the same, but
the warp and woof are red and white instead of being brown
and white.

Whilst we are on the subject of colours, I would observe
that it seems to be an almost invariable rule that primitive
peoples, as soon as they learn the use of them, adopt what
were considered not many years ago the three primitive
colours—viz., red, blue, and yellow, in their embroideries,
dress, and ornaments.   Recently, however, certain scientific
men have decided that this is a mistake, and that red, green,
and violet are the primary colours.

In the Himâlayas the people of Spiti and of Ladakh
know only of red carnelian, coral, turquoise, and amber as

ornamental gems. The dress of the women in the former
country reproduces these three colours only,—though some
of the richer women in Ladakh introduce small squares of
green cloth alternately with red ones on the square piece
of sheep-skin with the wool on, which they wear on their
shoulders both in summer and winter. Again, the same
combination of red, blue, and yellow is seen on old Norwegian peasant embroideries ; their colours and patterns
recall those now executed by peasant women in Albania.
These latter affirm that they use no set designs ; they
produce them, as it were, out of their own inner consciousness.

I would give in this place another remarkable instance
of the presence of the same two designs in conjunction,
occurring amongst widely separated peoples. In Dr Hans
Hildebrand's *South Kensington Handbook of Scandinavian
Art,* page 114, fig. 101, some silver beads are represented,
which, he states, belonged to a necklace found in Gothland
in a bronze vessel, together with a great treasure of bracelets,
pendants, etc., and coins, no one of which was struck after
1000 A.D. The centre bead has the so-called rat's tooth
raised work upon it, and those on either side of it are
ornamented with raised filigree scroll work. Singular to
relate, on a massive gold bracelet in the writer's possession—
bought some years ago, when an Arab Kâïd or native
Governor in Algeria was exchanging some native for French
jewellery—these same two designs are present side by side.
This bracelet is known to be the work of people living
beyond the Niger—in fact in the country explored by Mungo
Park. Can this be a coincidence—an accident ? Should

we not rather acknowledge that those who made the beads and the bracelet were in ages long past—of the same stock? The gold work of these people is very rarely met with, even in North Africa.   A specimen of the size of this bracelet was deemed almost unique by one who had a special knowledge of the subject.

In the *Folk Lore Journal*, Vol. V., parts 3 and 4, is an account of dances witnessed by us in various lands. Amongst others are descriptions of the secular and religious dances of Ladakh in Western Tibet.   The latter are performed only by Lamas or Buddhist monks.

A short paragraph from one of those papers furnishes another illustration of the survival of certain Asiatic customs in Europe which do not come under the special subjects to be treated further on.   It runs thus : " The monks when dancing are attired in a variety of costumes, composed of the most magnificent Chinese stuffs, stiff with embroidery.   Each man wears a gigantic headpiece made of thin board or *papier maché*. It comes down as far as his shoulders. Some of these masks are ornamented with fruits and flowers, modelled at least twice their natural size, and painted in brilliant colours.   They execute several different dances. In one, two Lamas are dressed up to represent a Chinese mandarin and his wife ; in another the two actors who come last upon the scene wear masks resembling ferocious-looking dogs.   One of these places himself against the entrance door, the other guards the door of exit for the performers.   These figures remind one of the Dwârpâlas or doorkeepers whose statues are frequently seen placed as guards on each side of the shrine of some old Hindû temple, as, for instance, at the so-called Seven Pagodas near Madras, and in other parts of Southern India."

Again, amongst the Buddhists of Ceylon a certain class of people are styled devil dancers. Specimens of various masks, said to be still used by them in their incantations or divination ceremonies, are now in the museum at Colombo. These masks are supposed to illustrate different phases of illness or bodily discomfort ; they represent, for instance, persons suffering from dumbness, from a strong attack of fever, from the feeling that a sick person is a devil or a god, from lameness, from a difficulty of breathing, from curious noises in the ears, from blindness, from insufferable heat, from a shivering fit, from a fit of partial hysteria, etc., etc.

In the Austrian Tyrol in the middle ages, and even down to forty years ago, it was the custom at Sterzing and at other places during Carnival time to act what were then styled " Teufel's Comödien," or Devil Comedies. Some of these plays (which in their nature belong to the class of *Moralities* rather than to the earlier forms of the Christian drama called Mysteries and Miracle plays) have been published from the original manuscripts in the quaint German of the beginning of the sixteenth century.

It would appear that the actors were in the habit of donning grotesque attire, as is still done in our Plough Monday celebrations in some parts of England. In the so-called Ferdinandeum or Museum at Innsbruck are some of the Teufel's Masken which were used on these occasions ; they are either of thin wood or of *papier maché*. One of them is especially curious. It came from the Oetz valley, and is known to have been used about forty years ago. Its great interest for us lies in that this mask is an embodiment of Indian and Central Asian symbolism. In type and character it is the counterpart of the masks above described as being worn by certain of the Lamas of Tibet in their religious dances; it almost exactly resembles those worn by the doorkeepers or Dwârpâlas who guard the entrance and exit of the courtyard in which these dances took place at Léh, where we saw them.

The Tyrolese mask has the large projecting eyes, the wide mouth with the huge pendant tusks (which are so familiar to us in connection with Chinese art), large ears, like those of the horse or the ass, between which are fixed a pair of ibex horns, and between these again is a serpent's head looking upwards. The tail of the reptile is seen coming out of the mouth of the mask. On the forehead, in front of the ears and horns, is a kind of coronet, formed of a succession of *triśuls* or tridents. From one side of this coronet issues a miniature dragon, and from the other a tiny serpent. On the left side of the mouth is a frog, which is evidently trying to seize the serpent's tail. The frog, the serpent, and the triśul or trident are all associated with Hindû Śaiva worship at the present day.

In the Tyrolese play, the nether limbs of the wearer of this mask were encased in pantaloons made of a coarse linen material dyed black and painted with tongues of flame, the folds of a large stuffed snake of the same material encircled his body and legs, being attached to a cloak of similar stuff which hung from his shoulders. When this singular costume had ceased to be used, owing to the discontinuance of these performances for the last forty years, it fell into the hands of a blacksmith, who must have been possessed of some dry humour: he had constructed a mechanical figure which he made use of to blow the bellows of his forge, he dressed it up in this attire, telling his neighbours that he thus "made the devil to work for him." An antiquarian, chancing to pass that way, saw and rescued these curious objects and placed them where they now are.

To quote another singular *rapprochement* between East and West: the Siamese are well known to be great tea-drinkers; when friends come to see them, tea is invariably placed before them. In that country it is considered the greatest breach of etiquette to refuse anything that is offered one: therefore when a guest has had sufficient, he should invert his cup on the saucer, since if it were left in its ordinary position the host would not fail to help him again, and good manners would oblige him to drink its contents. Also in Siam, the host or the hostess never quite fills a cup, since their guest might think it was only for once, and that he was not expected to go again to that house.

It is very remarkable to find this same custom continuing among the lower orders in England. Our village children, when at school feasts, may be observed to follow the same rule when they have had enough.

CHAPTER II

SUN WORSHIP

SUN-WORSHIP— probably the most ancient of all superstitions—still prevails in Hindostan. It had formerly a special existence in Phœnicia, Chaldea, Egypt, Mexico, and Peru. According to Allegre (*Hist. Comp. de Jesú*) the explicit worship of the sun, and more or less that of the other heavenly bodies—or at least a recognition of some supernatural power resident in or connected with them—was widely spread throughout Mexico, among both the uncivilised and the civilised tribes or peoples. In civilised Mexico, the sun was definitely worshipped under the name of Tomatink, or the sun in his four motions. Sometimes he was represented with a human face, surrounded with rays, sometimes by a full-length human figure. When they fought a battle, they endeavoured to take all their captives alive in order to reserve them for a solemn sacrifice to the Sun on great festivals. The victim was slain, his heart offered to the Sun, and then cast down before an idol.

The two most ancient and important Rajput races in India were denominated Sûryavaṁśa and Chandravaṁśa, or children of the Sun and the Moon.

In Hindostan this latter is a male deity. In the *Asiatic Researches*, Sir William Jones alludes to the universal adora-

14

tion of the solar orb, and says that the first dynasties of the Peruvian kings were dignified, like those in India, by the name of the Sun and the Moon.

When an eclipse of the moon is expected, many of the natives of Hindostan hasten down to the nearest river or tank and remain in the water the whole time of its duration, imagining that some dire misfortune would befall them were they to omit to do so. This Indian superstition probably took its rise in the idea that one should not look at this phenomenon directly, but indirectly—that is to say, one should not contemplate the luminary itself at such times, but regard only its reflection in the water.

There is a Hindû verse to the following effect : " Man dreads a crooked thing—the demon Râhu dares not seize the moon till he sees her full." They consider the eclipse to be caused by the demon Râhu seizing the moon in his mouth. Offerings of money for pious uses made during eclipses and when the sun enters the sign of Capricorn are deemed by them especially meritorious. In the *Antiquarian Repertory*, 1807, E. Jeffrey states : " In Scotland generally, and particularly amongst Highlanders, it is the custom for the women to make a curtsey to the new moon." He goes on to say : " Our English women, too, have a touch of this, some of them sitting astride a gate or stile the first evening the new moon appears, and saying, ' A fine moon, God bless her.' The like," he adds, " I have also seen in Herefordshire."

In *Herefordshire Words and Phrases*, by the late Rev. F. Havergal, it is stated " that it was formerly the custom in that county on the occasion of an eclipse for the common people to fill a bucket with water, place it where the sun's

reflection could be seen in it, and thus to watch its course."
The similitude between this and the Hindû idea is most
remarkable.

An apparent remnant of Sun-worship, engrafted on our
Christian practice, prevails in County Tipperary, Ireland.   It is
said the people are in the habit of placing a bucket of water
outside their house door on Easter morning.   When the vessel
is first placed there its contents are naturally much agitated,
and the people say that " the Sun is dancing on the water for
joy at the resurrection."

The Moon plays an important part in the Austrian Tyrol.
It is everywhere believed that she influences nature, therefore
nothing is done in either field, stall, house or wood, without
first consulting the moon.   Only at the wane of the moon is
the hair cut, in order that it may not grow again too quickly.

The Mexicans also have been described as being much
troubled and distressed at an eclipse of the Sun or Moon.
Some of the wild tribes regard the Sun and Moon as husband
and wife.   They believe that an eclipse of the Sun is caused
by domestic quarrels, and to soothe the ruffled spirit of the
Sun on such occasions the ruddiest human victims that could
be found used to be sacrificed to him.   For sacrifices to the
Moon under similar circumstances albinos were chosen.

The Comanches, a sub-division of the Apaches—a tribe
belonging to Northern Mexico—practise various religious
ceremonies, which are for the most part of a simple kind,
and addressed to the Sun as the great source of life.

According to Abbé Domenech, in his account of his
missionary labours, every Comanche wears a little figure of
the Sun round his neck, or has a picture of it painted on his

shield, whilst from his ears hang two crescents, which may possibly represent the Moon. To this day the *Key* (the symbol of Janus or the Sun) is used as a talisman by the lower orders in Naples. They call the Moon *Janara*, or, the wife of Janus. A woman will call another a Janara as a term of reproach.

Halhed (*Code of Gentoo Laws*, 1776) speaks of a spot in India, which in his day was much frequented by pilgrims— viz., Sûrya Kund in the Subah of Oudh. A festival was annually observed there called the Sûrya Pûjâ (or Sûrya-vrata). It took place on the seventh day of the bright half of the ninth month (January), when offerings of flowers were made to the Sun, and afterwards cast into the Ganges river. He also adds that the new-born babe of a Brahman was exposed to the solar beams.

Fire-worship as a special form of Sun-worship early prevailed in Persia, its votaries, the Magi, being forbidden to spit on the fire or pour water upon it, even if their dwellings or their goods were in danger of being consumed.

According to Hyde (*Religio Persarum*, p. 38), idolaters as well as these Sun-worshippers existed in ancient Persia, and the worship of fire and that of idols were combined at one period. Clement of Alexandria states that Artaxerxes, the son of Darius, caused idols to be made in human form for worship. He adds that this monarch was the first who caused statues to the goddess Venus to be made at Babylon, at Susa, and elsewhere.

The fire-worshipping Magi held the idolaters in abomination; but after the death of one of them, named Smerdis, the sect which opposed idols became extinct in Persia. Quintus Curtius, when describing the march of the army of Darius (writing, of course, long after its date) says that he was accompanied by an image of the Sun placed in a crystal, and the sacred fire was carried on a silver altar ; that the king's carriage was ornamented on all sides with images of gold and silver, and that there were also golden statues an ell in height on the top of it, one of which represented Bêlus (the Sun).   Tertullian in his *Apologia*, chap. xvi., gives us to understand that the Persians adored a figure of the Sun which they caused to be painted on canvas.   Zoroaster (Zardusht) assigned to Mithra, the Sun-god of the Persians, two principles, and made these exercise two distinct forces, each independent of the other, under the names of Ormuzd (good) and Ahrimân (evil). This in time, in the opinion of Mr Fiske (the American upholder of the Darwinian theories), produced the Manichæan heresy, in which the devil appears as an independently existing principle of evil ; and thus, in part at least, was continued the old Asiatic worship of the Sun in comparatively modern Europe.   " This heresy," says Mr Fiske, " was always ripe in Armenia ; it was through Armenian missionaries that Bulgaria was converted from heathenism, and from thence Manichæism penetrated into Servia and Bosnia, which latter was its headquarters from the twelfth century onwards, and was a perpetual thorn in the side of the Papacy."

The worship of the Persian sun-god Mithra penetrated to many places in ancient Italy.   As appears from an inscription found near the monastery of St Ambrose, at Milan, that spot was the site of Mithra's cavern or grotto and a seat of his sacrificing priests.   There is also a grotto on the island of Capri, in the bay of Naples, in which are the remains of a temple of Mithra. It is popularly called the grotto of Matromonia, but should be styled Mithramonia. In Naples itself, too, there was a temple to Mithra, the columns of which may still be seen in the church of Santa Maria à Cappella on the Chiatamone.

"The worship of Mithra was introduced into Italy after the return of Pompey the Great from his victories in Asia, and bears all the marks of dating from the second half of the last century of paganism. In fact, the Mithraic feasts and the mysteries of the god Mithra were established and recognised in Italy under the reign of Trajan, who was born 52 A.D., and ascended the throne 98 A.D. For nearly a century and a half the followers of Mithra were obliged, like the early Christians, to celebrate their religious rites in caves and grottoes, and the grotto of Mithramonia may be regarded as one of the spots where the votaries of this worship used to assemble in secret" (*Illustrazione Italiana*, March 1883).

Mithraic worship was not of long duration in Italy. It was tolerated and permitted by the Emperors in the first years of the second century of the Christian era; but Christianity was then already beginning to spread itself and gain ground, and was recognised by Constantine in the fourth century as the true and only State religion. According to ancient writers the ceremony of the initiation of a candidate into the Mithraic mysteries was very appalling. Tertullian says that the candidate encountered a drawn sword on the threshold of the cavern, from which, if he persevered in entering, he received more than one wound. He then had to pass repeatedly through the flames of a fierce fire, and undergo a rigid fast, which some have stated lasted fifty days, during which time he was to remain far from all human habitations; but this seems hardly possible : some kind of coarse food must have been permitted him. He was then beaten with rods for two whole days, and during the last twenty days of his trial was buried up to the neck in snow. If he endured all these privations and sufferings, the candidate was admitted as a disciple of Mithra, and a golden serpent was placed in his bosom, given him as a sign of his regeneration, for as the snake renews its vigour in the spring by casting its skin, so the vivifying heat of the Sun is annually renewed. Sokrates, the author of the *Ecclesiastical History*, who lived in the fifth century A.D., relates that in his time " the Christians of Alexandria, having discovered a cavern which had been consecrated to Mithra, but long closed up, resolved to explore it and see what remnants of that superstition it contained, when to their astonishment the principal thing they found in it was a great quantity of human skulls, with other bones of men that had been sacrificed. They were brought out and publicly exposed, and excited the utmost horror in the inhabitants of that great city."

It is not impossible that, to the people of Italy, Mithra was the Sun himself. He was not so to the Persians : to them he was only a satellite of the Sun, a powerful god, though not the first or the supreme one; in fact, more like a saint of our own days. The Persians adored Mithra, but only for the favours which they believed he could obtain for them by his intercession with the Sun.

Montfaucon, in his *Antiquities*, gives a description of a

statue—supposed to be that of Mithra—which was discovered
at Rome at the close of the sixteenth century, between the
Viminal and the Quirinal Hills. His account of it is taken
from that of an Italian sculptor named Vacca, who examined
the temple at the time it was excavated. The building was
circular, as were all the temples of the Sun and of fire. In
the centre was a statue of Mithra in white marble, rather
less than four feet in height. It stood erect upon a globe,
out of which issued a serpent, the emblem of life, twined in
numerous folds round the body of the god. The head of
the statue was that of a lion (one of the signs of the Zodiac),
its body that of a man. The hands were pressed close to the
breast ; they grasped two keys to indicate the god's solar
origin and his power over the two hemispheres. Around
him were suspended a circle of lamps in regular order : these
were apparently of baked earth. The most remarkable thing
regarding these lamps was that they were so arranged as to
turn the side which gave the light towards the statue. This
would seem to show that these ancient people knew that the
planets were opaque bodies, and derived their light from the
Sun, the central orb, around which they revolved. Winckelmann, in his work on Roman antiquities, gives a representation
of a bas-relief of white marble in the Casino of the Villa
Albani at Rome, which has been supposed to be a sacrifice to
the god Mithra. The central figure of this group is a youth in
the act of slaying a bull. He has flowing hair, and is attired
in a peaked or so-called Phrygian cap, a loose sleeved robe
reaching only to the knees, and confined at the waist with a
broad girdle. He has also tight trousers and pointed shoes,
such as are worn in Northern India at the present day. With

his left hand he grasps the head of the animal, with his right
he is thrusting a dagger into the flank of the bull, just above
the shoulder blade.   In the foreground a small dog is reaching
up to lick the wound; a serpent in an erect position seems to
be watching the course of the dagger ; near the serpent are
two scorpions.   Behind, and to the right of the principal
figure, is a half moon, within which is a human head and a half
bust with long flowing locks.   To the left of the central figure
is a large bird—a hawk or an eagle.   On the same side, but
still further to the left of the spectator, is another human head
of a more masculine character than the others, which may have
been intended for Mithra himself.   The worship of Mithra in
Europe was not confined to Greece and Italy, for the Greeks
introduced it into the south of France.   Arles is known to
have been a Greek colony : many of the inhabitants of that
city preserve to this day a Grecian type of features.   This
would seem to bear out what has been stated—viz., that
certain families in that place keep themselves apart from the
other inhabitants, and marry only amongst themselves.   We
have likewise evidence that the Romans introduced the Mithra-
cult into England.   In *Eboracum, or York under the Romans*,
published in 1842, C. Welbeloved gives an illustration and
description of several fragments of sculpture, undoubtedly of
Mithraic origin, which were found in and near the city of
York.   He also speaks of a Mithraic cave in Northumberland, discovered in 1821, which contained several interesting
remains pertaining to these rites.

    After this brief digression we will now return to Arles.
In the Museum at that place is a torso, or, technically speaking, a *Hermes* of white marble (Plate III., fig. 4), a most

striking piece of sculpture, called a statue of Mithra. The head, most unfortunately, is wanting, the neck and shoulders are those of a man, the arms are kept close to the body by the folds of an enormous snake; between the coils, which are three in number, several of the signs of the Zodiac are distinguishable.

The sculptures described above are most interesting and instructive. The presence of Zodiacal signs serves to show that Mithra was a Sun-god, and this assists in connecting the snake with Sun-worship: in each instance the serpent plays an important part. Sun, fire, and snake worship and their respective emblems are intimately bound up together; subtle links and fine gradations unite them in some cases almost insensibly.

Passing through the fire is an ancient heathen custom alluded to in 2 Kings xvii. 17. Those who were to be initiated into the mysteries of Mithra had to undergo this ordeal; Virgil says that the same practice was followed in the worship of Apollo by the Etrurians on Mount Soracte. Amongst other heathenish customs, St Chrysostom censures the custom of lighting two great fires and passing between them. Some have supposed that the Hebrews caused their children to pass between two fires, others are of opinion that they waved them about in the flames whilst the worshippers of Moloch leapt through the fire or danced around it. A somewhat similar ceremony, called *Dam Madâr*, is still very popular with the lower orders in Northern India, it consists in jumping into a fire and treading it out. It is performed with the view of securing immunity from snake bite and the stings of scorpions.   It takes its name from a certain man *Shaikh Madâr* of *Syria*, a great saint and reputed miracle worker ; he died in 1434 A.D.   Herklots, in his *Qanoon-e-Islam*, gives this ceremony in detail.   Several Indian gods and goddesses are known under more than one name, according to the qualities and attributes with which they are invested—*e.g.*, one of their names for *Pârbati*, the wife of Śiva, is *Kâlî*: she is then represented and believed to be a bloodthirsty and revengeful goddess, and they consider it acceptable to her that they should walk on the fire ; and when they are ill they address her in these words : " O Kâlî, only cure me, and I will walk on fire in your holy presence."

In Normandy, Brittany, and even in the British Isles, traditional usages are still observed which serve to connect Fire with Sun-worship.

On Midsummer Eve, at Trondhjem in Norway, bonfires are lighted at sunset on the hills near and around that city.   At that time of the year the sun sets about 11.20 P.M. ; the whole population turns out to assist at the ceremony of kindling the fires.   A strong pole is driven into the ground, a barrel is then fixed upon it and filled with shavings and other combustible materials, its position being most carefully adjusted, so that it may point exactly to that part of the horizon where the Sun will set on that day.

In England, the 21st of June, or the longest day, used to be a great day at Stonehenge, and is said to have occasionally degenerated into a disorderly assemblage.   It was formerly the custom for a large number of persons to assemble there at dawn, in order to watch for the rising of the Sun, which on this particular day can be seen from the centre of the circle of Stonehenge coming up exactly over the centre of a large stone at some distance from the rest, called the " Pointer" stone, striking its first rays through the central entrance on to the so-called altar stone. This custom has been quoted by one writer as an obvious proof of Sun-worship in the original constructors of the circles, and he adds the statement that at noon on the same day, the "pointer" stone appears as though set at an inclination similar to that of the gnomon of a sun-dial.

In the province of Connaught and in other parts of the South of Ireland, it is still the custom to kindle fires on St John's Eve : they are kept up till sunrise. A friend (since deceased) who, when quartered in Ireland, had frequently been an eye-witness of this scene, told the writer that on such occasions mothers are in the habit of giving their young children a kind of baptism of fire. He himself had had infants thrown to him through the flames—not once only, but many times. The people call this ceremony Baal-tine-glas or Baal-fire-blue. The term Baltinglass (now extinct except as an Irish place-name) is a corruption of these words. The women, this officer added, prefer asking gentlemen to catch their children, thinking possibly that they will be more gentle with them than one of their own class in life. He also said that he had quite recently made inquiries as to whether this custom still survived, and was answered in the affirmative. At Youghal, County Waterford, the inhabitants light numerous wood fires in different parts of the town every year on St

John's Eve. Each person, or one member of each family, seizes a burning brand and runs with it to his house. If he arrives at his dwelling with his torch alight, it is an omen that the ensuing year will be a happy and prosperous one to him and his ; but should it be extinguished, some dire calamity will, he thinks, fall upon his family. The new brand is then put in the place of honour above the hearth (the sacred spot in all ages and with all peoples), and that of the previous year removed and burnt.

LE RETOUR DU SOLEIL.

The following account of a festival called Le Retour du Soleil, said to have been performed at Les Andrieux, in Dauphiné, is a translation of a rather curious, and now, we believe, rare book, entitled *Histoire des Hautes Alpes*, by Baron Ladoucette, a former prefect of this department under the first French Empire, who states that he himself witnessed this fête. Mons. Ladoucette's work was published in the latter part of the first quarter of the present century.

Desirous of ascertaining whether "le Retour du Soleil" was still kept up at Les Andrieux, a friend in Grenoble was applied to : the reply seemed to throw doubts upon the authenticity of this festival as a relic of antiquity. My informant's reply was as follows :—

"An individual named Ferrand, who was a Councillor of the Prefecture under Baron Ladoucette, left memoirs behind him, which have caused some persons to doubt the genuineness of Baron Ladoucette's account," but, he adds, " M. Ferrand probably did this in order to gain for himself the reputation of a *bel esprit*."

In his memoirs the Councillor states that it was he who imagined and caused this festival to be performed, and that he did so in order to impose upon the credulity of Baron Ladoucette, who, as he knew, was then compiling his work. This version of what was, if committed, a cruel practical joke, has been accepted by MM. Chaper and J. Roman ; the latter, however, qualifies his acceptance of this view by adding that the oldest inhabitants of Les Andrieux are convinced that their ancestors always celebrated this *fête*, and that, of those to whom he spoke, many were alive in the time of Mons. Ferrand and would in consequence have been perfectly competent to state whether this ceremony only took its rise under his administration. On the other hand, Elisée Reclus, in his *Géographie Universelle*, speaks of this festival as a very ancient one. Baron Ladoucette's story runs as follows :—

"On the banks of the river Severaise, in that portion of the High Alps which was formerly called the Godemar valley, is a little hamlet called Les Andrieux.

"During the space of one hundred days in winter the inhabitants of this valley do not see the sun. Only on the 10th of February is this orb once more visible to them, therefore on this particular day, as soon as dawn appears, four shepherds make the round of the village, and by sounding pipes and trumpets, they announce to the inhabitants that the festival is about to commence. They then go to the house of the oldest inhabitant of that place, who, under the title of *Le Vénérable*, presides at the ceremony of saluting the return of the sun.

"At 10 A.M. all the villagers, each provided with an

omelette, assemble on the *Place* of the village. A deputation preceded by the shepherds then goes to fetch *Le Vénérable*, and accompany him to the place of meeting, where he is greeted with loud acclamations. *Le Vénérable* places himself in their midst, announces to them the object of the fête, and then,—each holding his plate with an omelette upon it,—they form a chain and dance a *farandole* round him.[1]

" As soon as the dance is at an end, *Le Vénérable* gives the signal for departure ; and, as before—preceded by the shepherds—all follow him to the stone bridge which is at the entrance to the village.[2] On reaching this spot, each one places his omelette on the parapet of the bridge, then all go into a meadow close by, where *farandoles* are once more danced until the sun appears overhead. As soon as this occurs, each person goes and takes up his omelette, which he offers to the sun. *Le Vénérable* also, bareheaded, does the same. As soon as the solar rays illumine the whole village, all return thither, escorting *Le Vénérable* to his house. They then disperse to their respective homes, where they eat their omelettes. This festival lasts the whole day ; it sometimes extends even into the night."

[1] An intelligent bookseller at Grenoble, when asked to describe a *farandole*, said, that any joyous movement executed by peasants in the open air was styled a *farandole* in that part of the country.

[2] A Grenoble correspondent wrote in 1887-88 that this bridge, though in ruins then, still preserved the name of *Pont de L'Omlette*.

CHAPTER III

SUN AND MOON (OR CUP) SYMBOLS

SUN and moon (or cup) markings and fire symbols are very intimately connected with each other ; it is difficult to separate them.

We propose now to treat of certain sun symbols and of customs connected with solar worship with which the element of fire is also occasionally associated. To the Svastika, which is more especially a fire emblem, will be devoted a separate chapter.

In all parts of the world we find traces of sun worship having existed amongst races of apparently different origins.

A verse in the *Rig-Veda* called the *Gayatrî* was esteemed by the ancient Hindûs to be the noblest verse in the Vedas. The *Gayatrî* is addressed to the sun. It occurs in the *Rig-Veda*, iii. 62.10. As given by Colebrooke in the *Asiatic Researches*, the words are :—

" *Tat savitar-varenyam bargo dêvasya dhîmahi : dhiyo yô nah prachodayât.*" He translates this : " Earth, sky, heaven, let us meditate on these, and on the most excellent light and power of the generous sportive and resplendent sun, praying that it may guide our intellects." [1]

[1] Prof. H. H. Wilson's abridged translation of this verse runs thus in his *Vishnu Purâna*, Vol. II., pp. 250-255 : " Let us meditate on the sacred light of the divine sun that it may illuminate our minds." In his *Rig-Veda*, Vol. III., p. 110, he

In the first or Vedic era of the history of India, sun-worship occupied no inconsiderable place in the religion of the Hindûs. An old Marâthâ Brahman from Pûnâ once told the writer that the Śaivas worship the sun even now.

The all-covering Varuna (Ouranos, or god of the Heavenly regions of the Greeks) was originally among the Persians the god of the clouds, of the celestial sea, and of the heavens above it. When this branch of the Aryans reached Southern India, he became the god of the earthly sea, which they then saw for the first time. The sun, while it was still regarded as a wheel, a store of gold, an eagle, a falcon, a horse, etc., was also styled the eye of Varuna. To the Germans and the Anglo-Saxons the Sun was the eye of Woden. In the north of Asia, Mithra was associated with Varuna. Mithra was the god of daylight; he and Varuna were fabled to sit together on a golden throne and journey at even in a brazen car; thus from the horse-sun and the wheel-sun was naturally developed the chariot and the divine charioteer. Euripedês gives the sun a winged car; on coins from Eleusis, Dêmêtêr is represented riding in such a car drawn by two serpents. The serpent, as we shall see later on, was an element in sun-worship, and was used in connection with the Mithraic mysteries.

At Hindû marriages in Kumâon, in the Central Himâ-

---

afterwards varied this version to : " We meditate on that desirable light of the divine Savitri (*i.e.*, the sun) who influences our pious rites."

Major R. C. Temple is of opinion that Benfey has more accurately rendered it thus : " May we receive the glorious brightness of this the generator of the god who shall prosper our works," and adds that most Sanskritists have tried their hands at this verse. It was, he says, more than probably meant originally as a mere invocation to the sun.

layas, it is customary for the *Púrohit* (family priest) to worship the fire and read the marital vows. These are repeated separately by the bride and the bridegroom, each agrees to live with the other in harmony, they making the fire and the sun their witnesses (*Panjab Notes and Queries*, Vol. II, note 244). The Kôls of Sambalpûr in the Central Provinces are sun-worshippers, as are also the Kurkûs of the Mahâdêo hills, more than 400 miles to the north-west of that place. The Khônds, an aboriginal race, classed as Dravidians, combine faith in the sun and in mother earth.

From the earliest times it has been customary to turn to the east in worship. In India many temples have been built with the object of causing the rising sun to throw its first rays upon the entrance, and thus illumine the god or the stone in its innermost shrine, which at other times would be in almost total darkness. In Maisûr and in the Salem district are some remarkable kistvaens or tombs, supposed to be those of a prehistoric race. They are, I believe, round-headed slab-stone monuments. Attention was first drawn to them by Col. Welch in the early part of this century, but they were almost forgotten till Lieut.-Col. Branfill of the Trigonometrical Survey re-described them a few years ago. Each tomb is surrounded by round-headed slabs of gneiss, some of which are as much as fourteen feet in height. What may be termed the tomb proper consists of an ordinary kistvaen made of six slabs of gneiss. One forms the roof, another the flooring, and the other four the sides of the tomb. It invariably faces the east, and the slab on that side always has a hole in it. In most cases the aperture is about fifteen inches in diameter, but in some instances it is not more than **two** inches across. The stones which compose the tomb are arranged thus :

It seems not impossible that this arrangement may have had some connection with the *Svastika*. The eastern position given to the door of the Hindû temple, and the eastern aspect of the entrance to these tombs, was in the former case possibly intended to signify that from the sun came light, warmth, and fertility ; and in the latter case to typify that as the sun rose (was new born) each day, so the soul of man received a new birth. All savage and semi-civilised races seem to have an idea that when the body dies there is some kind of future existence for the spirit of man. Lastly, we modern Christians perpetuate this custom of Orientation in the position given to our Churches, and in turning to the east when we recite the creeds or general assent to the articles of the Christian faith.

In an article on this subject in the *Antiquarian Repertory*, 1807, E. Jeffrey writes : " In days of yore, when a church was to be built it was customary to watch and pray on the vigil of the dedication, and to take that point of the horizon where the sun rose the following morning *for the East*, which makes that variation so that few stand true, except those built between the two equinoxes." He adds : " I have experimented some churches, and have found the line to point to that part of the horizon where the sun rises on the day of the Saint to whom the church is dedicated."

In European common life also, when passing the wine, or dealing a pack of cards, we constantly hear it said that this should be done "the way of the sun," and some persons deem it most unlucky if, through inadvertence, the bottle be sent round the other way (or from right to left).

Taking it all in all, it may be broadly laid down that in Europe sun, moon, and fire symbols are more numerous in northern lands than in southern ones. In the inclement regions of the north, light and warmth would be considered the greatest of blessings. Sun and cup symbols first appear in Scandinavia on objects which have been classed as belonging to the later stone age. At this period (as far as is hitherto known) they were of two kinds only—viz., the ring cross for the sun, and the cup-shaped hollow for the moon : both generally recognised as emblems of warmth and fertilizing power. The former have been found in extraordinary numbers in the so-called bog and grave finds both in Norway and in Denmark (see Plate I, figs. 1 to 16).

The late Kaṁer Herr Dr Worsaae, head of the Archæological Department in Denmark, who gave much attention to this subject, came to the conclusion that the single ring cross was the Sun-god himself; and the Svastika and its outcome, the three-armed cross (the triquetra or triskele), another of the principal gods of the Northern triad; and, finally, that the stars became emblems of the sun itself or of the large heavenly bodies.

Plate I, fig. 17, is a design taken from a vase of

coarse pottery in the museum at Copenhagen belonging to what has been called in Scandinavia the later Bronze Age. In the centre is a wheel (the chariot wheel of the sun?), and below it is a quaint two-headed mythical animal, which may have been intended to represent the sun-snake (or lightning), which, from its zig-zag, serpentine form, might naturally be likened to a snake, and thus become associated with both fire and solar worship. When we come to speak more particularly of the Svastika, we shall see that one form of this fire symbol is but a degenerate kind of serpent. On ornaments belonging to the later Bronze Age we find the wheel-cross—considered to be an emblem of the chariot which, according to the most ancient beliefs throughout Asia and Europe—the sun was supposed to drive through the sky. Now, both in Holland and Denmark it is no unusual circumstance to see a waggon wheel on the roof of a stable or other building, placed there with the object of inducing a stork to build its nest upon it. No doubt the red legs of this bird caused it to be regarded as a fire fowl. It is a welcome guest; it comes with the spring, and departs before the winter; it is the bringer of warmth and of fine weather.

In the Grand Duchy of Baden waggon wheels may be seen on the towers of many churches, and on the tops of high houses or barns. A landowner in a small village close to the Swiss frontier told the writer that a stork's nest on a building prevented the roof from being blown off by high winds; an innkeeper living close by gave the usual version, " that the stork preserves from fire and brings good luck." In Hesse the same belief is current. In Asia the wheel is associated with Buddha ; it is an emblem which occurs frequently on Buddhist coins and on Buddhist architecture. In Buddhist writings Buddha is spoken of as turning the wheel of the law, or preaching. On Plate I, fig. 33, is a representation of a Buddhist wheel in the writer's possession ; it came from a ruined mané in Lahûl. It is a stone disc, about ten inches in diameter by one inch in thickness. Tibetan characters occupy the spaces between the spokes of the wheel, but as the stone is rather worn, it is not easy to reproduce the letters very accurately ; it is clear, however, that the inscription is the well-known formula, "*Aum mani padmê hûm.*"

Sun and moon emblems, and the *Svastika* in the various forms which it assumed, continued to be used abundantly in Denmark and Norway on ornaments and objects in common use during the later Bronze Age and the earlier and middle Iron Ages. The same symbols occur also during the later Iron Age or Viking period. " Curiously enough, in the new Runic alphabet, which was there adopted at this time, the letter *S*, which recalls one of the old Sun symbols, was called *Sol* or *Sun*" (*Handbook of Danish Arts*, by the late Kamer Herr Dr Worsaae).

On Plate I, fig. 35, is represented a small cruciform tube of terra-cotta which was found in the cemetery belonging to the ancient salt mines at Hallstadt in Austria. The sun symbol engraved upon it appears to be a combination of the symbols in figs. 18 and 19 on the same plate, which come from Denmark. Fig. 34 is a copy of a silver brooch in the Historical Museum at Stockholm ; it is classed as belonging to the later Iron Age. This is a remarkably interesting object, since marks which are generally recognised as sun and moon (or cup) symbols, encircle a Svastika, or emblem of Fire.

Fig. 38 is a brooch belonging to the later Bronze Age (as regards Scandinavia, be it observed, in all cases). Sun and cup symbols are also prominent in this example. Two brooches, one of an exactly similar type, were found a few years ago in an ancient grave near Bregenz, on the Lake of Constance. The fact of these purely Norwegian ornaments being found so far south assists in confirming an idea which has long existed, that the three Swiss cantons of Uri, Schwytz, and Unterwalden were colonised by people from Scandinavia, who wandered thither in consequence of a famine in their own country. The inhabitants of a valley near Brientz, in canton Berne, have to this day a tradition that their ancestors came from Scandinavia.

Fig. 37 is a drawing of a crucifix bought at Bergen in Norway; a similar one in a museum is classed as being of the eleventh century—i.e., when Christianity was first introduced into those parts. It is of a peculiar type. It will be observed that three nails only have been used to fasten the body of the Saviour to the cross; the feet are crossed over each other; one nail pierces both. Sun symbols are pendant from it, which seems to show that in those early times the people were permitted by their teachers to combine their former worship with their new faith (as in Russia). A small brass cross of the same type, brought from Norway by a friend, retains the three pendants, but in this case the sun symbols are replaced by raised dots in the form of a cross.

Sun symbolism in Scandinavia has thus been brought down to about 1000 A.D.; but such symbols also exist there in museums on objects classed as belonging to the Middle Ages. In the museum at Bergen are some apparently mythical small animals of that period, which would seem to have been children's toys, with sun marks ⊙ on their bodies; and on an old Norwegian bridal crown, stated to have come from the Sogne fjord district, and referred to the same age, there are Sun and Moon symbols alternately with pendant Suns: its upper edge is finished off with cup marks.

Plate II is a representation of a wizard's drum from Lapland, now in the Norwegian Museum at Stockholm. Though the Laplanders are professedly Lutheran Christians, they still retain great faith in augury and divination. They are very superstitious, and if on going abroad in the morning they meet with an unlucky omen, they return home, and do not stir out again the rest of the day. It is said also that they still pray to their ancient idols for the increase and safety of their herds. Drums of this kind are used by their magicians to form prognostications; small brass rings are placed on different parts of its surface, and the drum being beaten with a small hammer, these rings dance upon the signs represented upon it, and the sorcerer, according to the course taken by them, and after going through certain manœuvres, professes to foretell events.

The Sun, the Moon, and certain of the planets are definable upon this drum; the meaning of the other symbols is not so apparent; some little animals, like rats, would seem to be worshipping the heavenly bodies.

Symbols and cup markings exist on the natural rock and on Megalithic monuments in India, in England, Scotland, and Ireland, and also in Brittany.

In November 1894, shortly before quitting Kashmir, after a fourth visit to that country, the writer's attention was attracted to the remains of certain old buildings composed of large hewn stones, situated about a mile distant from the European quarter of Śrînagar. On a closer inspection, one of these buildings proved to be a ruined Muhammedan so-called *Ziârat* or walled enclosure, in which is the tomb of some saint. A few yards distant are low walls of a similar character. According to some natives living near, this latter was formerly a Mosque.

Directly in front of the *Ziârat*, and placed in a sloping position against a rough wall, which had possibly originally been its outer enclosure, is a singular stone, which we may venture to say could never have belonged to either of the above-named buildings. It is almost circular, but on accurate measurement it proved to be (allowing for a small portion which had been broken off) four feet in diameter one way, and four feet four inches the other. The thickness of this slab is about ten inches. The under or back side is very roughly hewn; its upper surface is carefully smoothed hewn work. All round the stone, at a distance of an inch and half from the edge, is a distinct trench, three inches and a half in width. Within this area, scattered over the surface, are numerous depressions (so-called cup markings) more or less carefully made, and similar to those hollowed stones which, if found in Brittany, in the island of Guernsey, in Cornwall, Scotland, or Ireland, would be styled prehistoric cup markings.   Four of these depressions are of considerable size, being at least three inches in diameter, and two inches in depth.   They are remarkably well defined.   There are also several smaller cup-marks, some not so deep or so distinct as the others.   The natives on the spot say that this stone is old old—centuries old ; that it has never been used for any purpose by either themselves or their progenitors, so far as their traditions carry them.   They appeared, however, to regard it with a kind of veneration, as an object whose use and origin was unknown to them.   Indeed, its general character and appearance would seem to point to an earlier stage of civilisation than any remains we have ever yet seen in Kashmir.

There is a most striking resemblance in form and type between some of the ancient rock sculptures in the Kângra valley and in Kumâon, N.W.P. India, and the marks on various sculptured rocks at Patrickstown, Knockrath, and Slieve na Cailliagh in Ireland.   On some of these stones two of the chief emblems of the worship of the Hindû god Śiva are unmistakably present.   Plate III, fig. 2, is a reduced drawing of the cap-stone of a chamber or small dolmen formed of unhewn stones, and existing at Baker's Hill, Ross-shire.   The incised marks upon it recall both Sun and Moon symbols.   Stones with cup markings have also been found near Inverness by Wm. Jolly, F.S.A.Scot., H.M.'s inspector of schools, who thus describes them : " Whispers are not uncommon in that district that the so-called *basin stone* near Arpafedie, and not far from Kessock Ferry, possesses hidden virtues similar to those of the font at Killianan on Loch Ness, and other stones ; childless women bathe in its cloud-drawn waters immediately before sunrise.

St Columba's font, near Abriachan, Inverness, is a hollow stone basin, which is said to have been used by St Columba himself for baptism when he visited King Brude in his castle near Inverness, and it goes by his name. It seems to be thought also to possess other virtues ; amongst these, the water it contains is held to have salutary effects in connection with child-bearing ; women are said to have frequented it with this object till very recently. It seems a debatable point whether the basin and circular channel are really ancient or ecclesiastical, some thinking that this stone was intended for a mill-stone ; however, the people hold that when emptied by any one, the basin fills again of its own accord. Experiments made by the uninitiated sceptic do not confirm this belief. The indisputable fact nevertheless is, that even in the hottest weather it is generally filled with water. As a rule, Sun and Moon symbols would seem to be rare in the British Isles, but at New Grange, Drogheda, Ireland, is the accompanying supposed Sun symbol. Curiously enough in the Museum at Grenoble, dep. Isère, France, amongst the collection of Gallo-Roman antiquities found in that neighbourhood, is a highly-finished group in bronze. At one side is a lion's head and fore-paws. The action of the animal is very spirited—it appears to be springing forward from right to left. In a line with the lion, but facing the other way, is the partially veiled bust of a woman in the Greek style. Beyond this again is a horse led by a man dressed in the short tunic worn by slaves in Roman times, and on the horse's flank is precisely the same symbol as that figured above from New Grange, Ireland. The horse stands on a kind of pedestal, on which is the inscription STRATILATES in Roman characters. It is a curious fact, and one perhaps not generally known, that certain women in Albania tattoo their arms and foreheads with the Sun symbols common to the later Bronze Age in Scandinavia. When in Corfu in 1883 I observed the mark figured on Plate I, fig. 4, on the centre of the forehead of more than one Albanian woman—(one of the caste marks of India is similar to this), and also figs. 23, 25, and 26 tattooed on the arms and wrists of some of these people, who, about six years previously, had been allowed to settle on that island after several of their villages had been burnt by the Turks and many of their inhabitants massacred.

Another variety of cup markings existing both in England, Guernsey, Scotland, and in Brittany, also finds its counterpart in Kumâon on the natural rock. The number of some of these depressions on particular stones may possibly have some connection with Hindû planet worship.

Plate III, fig. 3, depicts a menhir from Brittany, which forms one of a line of monoliths (alignements, as they are there called). These " lines " are sometimes composed of as many as ten parallel rows of such stones. They may occasionally be traced for two or three miles, and usually—if not invariably—terminate in a dolmen or prehistoric tomb made of unhewn stones, or in a mound containing several dolmens. Antiquarians seem to be agreed in regarding them as the tombs of chiefs. The menhirs may have served as avenues to indicate the road to the tomb, or have been looked upon as sentinels guarding the approach to it, for fragments of burnt and imperfectly calcined bones have been found beneath many of them. Might these not be the remains of slaves or retainers who sacrificed themselves, or were sacrificed, at the burial of their chief? According to the Hindû reckoning there are nine planets. These are worshipped daily in their special temple at Benares, under the name of the *Naugraha*, or the *Nava Graha*. It is most interesting to find this same number *nine* as cup-marks on stones which evidently belong to the pre-historic age. In the first part of the late Rev. W. C. Lukis' *Pre-historic Monuments of the British Isles*, embracing those of Cornwall only, mention is made of a stone monument near St Keverne, now locally called "the three brothers of Grugrith." To use Mr Lukis' own words, " This monument is remarkable on account of its construction. A massive stone of irregular shape, 8 feet by 5 feet, is supported on two stones. One of these is 8 feet 6 inches long, and nearly 5 feet broad, and appears to be a rock *in situ*, and to have been selected on account of its suitableness ; the other is a slab 7 feet 9 inches broad, and 18 inches thick. It is set up on edge, 2 feet 6 inches from, and parallel to, the former. The remains of a mound are still visible." This monument is given on Plate IV, fig. 1. As regards the present paper, the chief interest attached to it concerns the cup-marks, which are nine in number, eight on the capstone and one on the rock. In this they coincide with those on the stone on Plate III, fig. 1 (actual size) found at Kerhan near Arradon, above two miles from Vannes in Morbihan and now in the Museum at Vannes. The nine cup-marks upon it would seem to have been arranged on some special plan ; from its size it might have been a house altar.

Plate IV, fig 2, represents a cup-marked stone standing by the roadside in the Forest Parish, Guernsey. Six hollows only are now visible above ground, but it is not unreasonable to suppose that others exist below, though it is not easy to ascertain the fact, since this monolith borders a hard metalled road. Fig. 3 on the same plate is a drawing of a dolmen called La Garenne, situated on L'Ancesse Common, Guernsey. Here again we have nine cup-marks, which may have been intended to symbolise the sun and the moon and the other seven planets (according to the Hindû and probably pre-historic reckoning). The regularity of their arrangement seems to indicate that some meaning was attached to these symbols. Fig. 1, plate I., has been found in Savoy and also in Wales.

The cross with cup-marks round it exists on a sepulchral urn found in Wales, and the cross with supposed sun and moon symbols on a fragment of pottery at Villanova in Italy. Fig. 23 on the same plate is at the bottom of a small drinking cup in the writer's possession, coming from Norway. It has the exact form of the Scottish quaigh—it has doubtless served as a measure for a dram of spirits ; and a silver spoon, purchased in Bergen, bears this mark. It is of a type said to be peculiar to that part of Norway, styled the Nord-land, a district north of Trondhjem, and extending beyond the Lofoden Islands.

Only within the last very few years has public attention been drawn to the fact that pre-historic cup-marked and inscribed stones are found in Switzerland. Those of the Rhone Valley in the Canton Valais would appear to have been especially studied by Mons. Reber and others.

Mons. Reber in 1890-91 was preparing a descriptive and illustrated account of certain of these monuments. Pending its publication, he sent some short articles on the subject to the *Journal de Genève*, in one of which he states that near Salvan (3035 feet), a village on the road between Châtelard and Vernayez, he found numerous pre-historic remains. Those on the " Rocher du Planet " would seem to be the most remarkable ones. On three rock terraces, rising one above the other at a distance of some metres apart, he counted 300 different sculptures grouped in nine divisions. These consist of so-called cup-marks or circular depressions, of lines, of circles, triangles, squares, and other symbols. A few years ago the late Dr F. Keller, the celebrated Zurich archæologist, published an account of two cup-marked stones found in the Val D'Anniviers, the one at St Luc (5495 feet), and the other at Ayer, no great distance off, and at the same altitude. In 1887 another cup-marked block was found when the ground was being prepared for the enlargement of the Bella Tola Hotel at St Luc.

Above the village of St Luc, is the so-called " Pierre des Sauvages " or Stone of the Savages. From time immemorial the people have given this name to an immense block of siliceous schist which has been broken into three large, and many smaller fragments. On the central block Mons. Reber says there are 200 round and oval cup-marks of various dimensions, sometimes joined to each other in twos and threes, by incised lines. On another block he found twenty very typical cup-marks.

In the Val de Moiry, the Western branch of the Val d'Anniviers, just above Gremenz, is a large erratic block

of stone on which are two impressions of a human foot.
When M. Reber went thither he found other pre-historic
symbols at this spot, *viz.*, twenty-four cup-marks arranged
in groups of two, four, or even seven joined together, also
some carefully sculptured signs, being combinations of
semi-circles, cup-marks, and lines bent at obtuse and at
right angles. To the west of this there is another large
block called by the inhabitants of this district, "*La Pirra
Martera.*" A tradition has been carried down from father
to son that Pagan worship was formerly conducted at this
spot, and that human sacrifices were held there. This
stone is an enormous erratic block of gneiss of a lozenge
form, it rests upon one angle, the top presents a sharp
point; it has cup-marks likewise, and on its S.-E. edge
is a group of various symbols similar in character to those
above described; they have been most carefully executed,
but are less deeply cut than the cup-markings. Somewhat less than thirty feet to the S.-E. of the Pirra Martera
is a rock with two parallel depressions in the form of a
human foot, they are ten inches long, and six inches and
half wide at the upper part.

Descending towards Gremenz there is another erratic
block, on which are some cup-marks and artificially made
lines; and again, near the little village of St Jean, between
Gremenz and Vissoye, is another stone with thirteen regular
cup-marks which are polished in the interior.

CHAPTER IV

SOME have held the Svastika to be an emblem of the Sun, and others, again, hold that the arms of the cross represent two pieces of wood and are typical of fire, which—as first produced by primitive peoples—resulted from two crooked sticks being laid one across the other, and a hole drilled through both; in this a pointed stick was then inserted, and rapidly twirled by the hands till all were ignited at the points of contact.[1] At the present day the sacred fire in Hindû temples is said to be kindled in this manner. Tylor (*Early History of Mankind*) mentions that the Eskimo kindle a new fire by a very similar process—they, most probably, see nothing sacred in the performance. The Hindûs do not, it appears, make use of this symbol in their temples, but it is very frequent on the exterior walls of their houses in parts of Hindûstan. It is also not uncommon for the native bankers and jewellers in their larger cities to have a Svastika impressed on their safes.

The Buddhists of Western Tibet, of China, and of Japan, also employ this symbol, and within the last few months only, it has come to the knowledge of the writer that the Muhammedans of Kashmir have adopted it ; for the Svastika has now been found—as an ornamental decoration possibly—

---

[1] For a full discussion of the Svastika, by Thos. Wilson, LL.D., see *Report of the U.S. National Museum* for 1894, pp. 757-1011.

46

on the old wooden so-called Habbakhorten Mosque, distant about three miles from the European quarter of Śrînagar and also at Ladû — about three miles below Avantipur, on a Ziârat or building enclosing the tomb of some Muhammedan saint or Pîr to which pilgrimages are made.

The Lama Monastery at Hemis in Western Tibet, not far from Léh the capital, has this year (1896) been en fête; the day after the curious Lama religious dances had taken place, the Treasure room of the Monastery was opened in the presence of the Joint Committee : it had been closed for nine years, and was then unsealed and sealed again. The seal used was a simple Svastika. The contents of this place proved to be dust, mould and old silk.

In 1876 when we were at Léh, the capital of Western Tibet, a caravan arrived there with carpets from Yarkand. We seized this opportunity of purchasing some genuine Central Asian carpets, and secured some on which the Svastika was introduced into the border (Plate VI, figs. 2 and 5, represent a portion of the border and the central medallion on one of our purchases). The border, we would venture to say, gives a hint as to the origin of the celebrated Greek Key pattern, the medallion is also very interesting, as the only instance we had hitherto met with, in which the Svastika had assumed the form of the double Sun Snake of Scandinavia (Plate I, fig. 29).

Some members of the Jaina sect, now considered as old as the Buddhist, adopt a Svastika of this form a combination of figs 3 and 19 on Plate I, as the emblem of *Suparswa* the seventh of their Tîrthankars or Holy men. At Pâlitânâ in Kâthiâwâr, one of their most famous places of pilgrimage, a part of the worship of the women, as we saw it, consisted in forming Svastikas with the fingers, using uncooked rice, on a low table or box placed at the entrance of the shrine where they worshipped, after which, on rising, a verse was sung by all the worshippers standing.

The Vedas prescribe the aśvattha (*pipal* or *ficus religiosa*) and the Śami (*acacia suma*) as the kinds of wood to be used in kindling the sacred fire.   In Southern India especially it is very common to see two trees planted together when young, so that when grown older their branches and foliage become entwined.   The Hindûs style this "marrying the trees."   In this manner tree-worship became in a way connected with fire-worship.   Both the Greeks and Romans down to a late period in their primitive history used the method above described of procuring fire.   They found that the lower part was best made of certain softer kinds of wood, such as ivy (*vitus sylvestris*), whilst the laurel, thorn, or other hard wood was to be pre-ferred for the trypanon or drilling stick.   The Hindûs are said to regard the making of fire by this process with great awe ; similar feelings were extended to the element itself by the ancient Persian Magi, who denoted fire—which they con-sidered the Father and first principle of all things (as Zardusht or Zoroaster had taught them)—by the word *Bap*—signify-ing "father."   The same doctrine was also inculcated by Anaxagoras, the Greek philosopher.   Their modern repre-sentatives, the Parsî priests of a famous fire temple in Gujarât, boast that they have cherished the sacred flame of the ancient Persians unextinguished for 800 or 900 years, *i.e.*, ever since their expulsion from Persia by the Muhammedans.

The Parsîs, however, maintain that they do not worship fire, and much object to be called Fire-worshippers; but they admit that from their youth up they are taught to face some luminous object when praying. It is the imperative duty of the House Mother in a Parsî family to see that the kitchen fire never goes out, *and it is expressly forbidden to any Parsî woman to extinguish a candle or a lamp.* They maintain that they look upon fire as upon other natural phenomena—viz., as an emblem of divine power; but they never ask assistance or blessings from it. Pure Fire-worship also exists among the modern Hindûs. Thus, it was formerly prohibited to all Hindûs to go beyond the Indus river, or rather, properly speaking, the Kâlâ Pânî, or Black Water—as they call the Indian (or indeed any) Ocean into which the Indus empties itself; but a Marâthâ Brâhman told us that this rule is now relaxed, and that Hindûs may do so, if on their return to Hindustân they worship *Agni* or *Fire*, saying certain prayers to it, and giving alms and a feast to the Brâhmans. The man who gave this information was in Government employ on a salary of £20 a month, and he added that if he ever went to Europe it would cost him about £100 to be re-admitted into his caste on his return, since this sum varies according to the income a man is known to possess. The writer has remarked the Svastika tatooed on the back of the hand of an apparently wealthy high caste native lady, but cannot recall having ever seen it in the interior of any comparatively modern temple or shrine, nor its present use by the Buddhists of Kunâwar, the Spiti Valley, or Ceylon; in ancient times this does not appear to have been the case, since the Svastika exists as a so-called Mason's mark on some of the stones of the famous Buddhist tope at Sârnâth near Benares, and it is twice repeated on stones in the interior of some cells surrounding the court-yard of the Lâl Darwâza or Red Gate Mosque at Jaunpûr.

The Buddhists would seem to have recognised the lines of the hand. A small statue in the Lucknow Museum, found at Muttra (properly Mathura) a few years since, represents Buddha with uplifted right hand in the attitude of preaching : on the palm of the hand, the lines of life, of head or intellect, and of heart or strong affections, are clearly defined.

It would appear that within the last few years only, the Svastika has been found on ancient Egyptian articles of common use, In the South Kensington Museum are sundry embroideries on stuffs of various qualities purporting to come from Upper Egypt. On one specimen, of which the material resembles our rough bath towelling, is a large Svastika of the Hindû type, worked in brown wool.

Together with other Hindû symbols and customs, which will be enlarged upon later on, Spain adopted the Svastika. On the occasion of a Hindû marriage it is customary to send presents of sweetmeats, etc., to the friends and relations of the contracting parties. These are placed on trays, and covered with embroidered cloths, the latter articles are returned to the donor after the gift has been removed by the person to whom it has been sent, who places a small piece of money on the tray for the servant who brought the present. A similar custom prevails in Spain (or did so till very recently) ; and on the occasion of a fête or naming day, cakes and sweetmeats, arranged in this same manner, are sent to friends. The writer possesses two or three of the embroidered cloths used in Spain for this purpose; they are of hand-spun linen, bordered with old lace; conventional flower designs and various wonderful looking animals are worked upon them in coloured silks and, like the Indian embroideries of the same nature, the work is precisely alike on both sides. One of these cloths has the Svastika many times repeated upon it. The same symbol was present also on an ordinary well worn pocket handkerchief at Granada; it formed its only ornamentation. Enquiries failed to procure such a one, or to ascertain where they were manufactured.

This kind of embroidery was evidently known in early Jewish times, for in the *Song of Deborah* (Judges v. 30) mention is made "of needlework of divers colours, of divers colours of needlework *on both sides*, meet for the necks of them that take the spoil."

The Svastika has been found in nearly every country in Europe. In a letter written a few years ago by Prof. Max Müller to Dr Schliemann, and quoted in the latter's work entitled *Ilium, or the Cities of Troy* (where this and also Sun-symbols have been found in great numbers), the Professor says—" It (the Svastika) has been found on Bishop's Island, near Königswalde on the right bank of the Oder; on a vase discovered at Reichersdorf near Gruben; a whole row of this emblem surrounds the pulpit of Saint Ambrose at Milan; in the Catacombs at Rome it occurs a thousand times; it is seen also on wall paintings at Pompeii; on a Celtic urn found at Shropham in Norfolk and now in the British Museum; also on ancient Athenian and Corinthian vases; on the coins of Leucas of Syracuse; and in the large mosaic in the royal garden at Athens. It is found in Hungary and in China, amongst the Ashantis, and in Yucatan." In China it is used as a mark on pottery made specially for the magistrates, it is also a potter's mark in Japan, it exists on pottery in the island of Cyprus: a specimen is in the Museum at St Germain in France.   It will be observed, that Prof. Max Müller speaks here of the Svastika as having been only once found in England; but since he wrote the above, numerous examples of it have been unearthed during the excavation of a Roman villa at Brading in the Isle of Wight ; a form of this symbol, known as the double Sun snake of Scandinavia is on an Ogham stone at Pen Arthur in South Wales. Several years later, Prof. Max Müller wrote :—" The discovery made by Prof. Percy Gardner, to which you refer in the *Athenæum* of August 13th 1892, that the name of the town Mesembria, the city of midday, is figured on some of the coins by **MEΣπ** is decisive as to the meaning of the Svastika in Greece."   He con- tinues :—

" An equally decisive discovery, however, was made some years ago by the late E. Thomas, who in his papers on the Indian Svastika and its Western counterparts, published in the *Numismatic Chron.* in 1880—Vol. xx. pp. 18-48 showed that the emblem of the Sun in motion—a wheel with spokes— was actually replaced by what we now call the Svastika : that the Svastika is, in fact, an abbreviated emblem of the Solar wheel with spokes in it, the tyre and the movement being indicated by the crampons."

When in Burma, we came across many of the Kachins and Shans, two races of semi-civilized peoples living near the banks of the upper part of the Irrawady river. Until a very few years ago, their existence was unknown to Europeans. On enquiry, we were informed that it is tolerably certain that the Shans came from the extreme North of Rajputana or from the Southern part of Central Asia about 800 years ago. The origin of the Kachins is said to be unknown, they have a slightly Mongolian type of features. Both these peoples are acquainted with the loom ; from traders, Chinese, Indian, and others, who go up the country in the so-called cargo boats, they purchase hanks of cotton of various colours in large quantities and weave their own dress materials. The Kachins employ a great mixture of colours, but as a rule red predominates. It is a startling circumstance to find these latter, together with other designs, introducing the symbol of the Svastika in their garments and articles of daily use. The Shan's dress is dark blue, with a very small admixture of other colours as stripes or bordering.

Another form of the Svastika known as the Fylfot, Gammadion or *crux gammata* was also in use in England in the so-called *cinque cento* period, it resembles two serpents entwined.

In the treasury of the Cathedral at Valencia in Spain are two splendidly embroidered altar frontals, said to have formerly belonged to the old Church of St Paul in London, and to have been sold into Spain by King Henry the VIII. On one of them, which depicts our Blessed Lord going to his crucifixion, a soldier of the Roman army or of one of their auxiliaries is holding a standard on which is a fylfot.

A Svastika with a Latin inscription upon it was found

in 1779 by Armelini in the new catacomb of S. Agnese at Rome; Rossi, the great Christian archæologist, says of it, that "this inscription belongs to the second century of our era," and adds, "perhaps this is the most ancient *crux gammata* that has ever been found on Christian monuments."

For obvious reasons, on Plate I. are given the Sun and Fire symbols proper to Scandinavia; on Plate V. are illustrations of some of the different forms and modifications which the Svastika assumed in other parts of Europe and in the East. Fig. 1 represents the Hindû form of this symbol; fig. 2 the Buddhist and Jain form, both taken from drawings in Sir George Birdwood's *Industrial Arts of India*. Fig. 3 is taken from a fragment of a Persian silk carpet now in the Museum at Gothenburg in Sweden. Fig. 4 is a mark on Japanese pottery; fig. 5, on porcelain said to be made only for magistrates in China. Figs. 6, 7, 10 and 11 are examples from Dr Schliemann's Ilium. Fig. 8 is on a slab of marble now in the Museum at Naples, and found in the catacombs beneath that city; and fig. 9 is a representation of the Trinacria or three-legged Man of the arms of Sicily: in the centre is a human face surrounded with rays. In the Manx Man, or emblem of the Isle of Man, the face and the (? Sun's) rays belonging to the Trinacria have disappeared, and only the three legs remain. It has been supposed by some that the Trinacria and the Manx-man[1] are but forms of the Svastika as a Sun and Fire symbol which in process of time has lost

---

[1] See *History of the Migration of the Triskelion from Sicily to the Isle of Man*, by John Newton.—*Athenæum*, Sept. 10, 1892, pp. 353, 354.

one of its arms; this same type became in Scandinavia
(see Plate I, figs. 12 and 15) what is there styled the
Triskele. Fig. 12 is taken from a fragment of pottery
found in what is believed to be a pre-Etruscan cemetery
at Bologna in Italy. The row of Svastikas, the warrior,
and the mythical animal have to all appearance been stamped
on the clay in this example whilst it was yet soft. Plate VI,
figs. 3 and 4, give the position and detail of a raised silver
ornament on a lance brought from Japan, a few years ago,
by the present Lord de Saumarez and placed in his Japanese
Villa in the Island of Guernsey. It is identical with a form
of the triskele figured in cut 164 in Kamer Herr Worsaae's
Handbook of Danish Art.

Plate V, fig. 14, is especially interesting; the Svastika
is seen surrounded with half moons in various positions:
it is copied from a mosaic pavement found at Gubbio in
Italy in 1882.

On comparing the results of the grave and bog finds of
Norway, Denmark, and Sweden, it would seem that the
Svastika is most rare in the last named, and most common
in Norway, and that Sun and Fire symbols became disused
in the two latter countries about the twelfth century: that
is to say, not long after the introduction of Christianity there;
whereas in Norway they still continue in use down to our
own times, though their signification is probably unknown
to the present generation.

The so-called "Mangling Stick" is still in common use
in Norway. It is made of a single piece of hard and highly
polished wood about 18 inches long, by 8 or 10 inches wide.
At one end is sometimes carved in complete relief a small

wooden horse which serves as a grip for the hand; or else the wood is hollowed out so as to leave a raised portion for the same purpose.   Its use gives collars and cuffs a much better appearance than the ordinary flat or box iron can produce.   A Mangling Stick, bearing the date 1809 (now in the Norwegian Museum at Stockholm), is covered with Svastikas of the double Sun snake type, an apparent proof that in Scandinavia this was deemed a fire-symbol.

On referring to Plate I, it will be seen from the examples there given that the *Svastika* gradually changed its form in those countries; that from the simple *hak kors* or hooked cross, the Svastika became the double snake, and finally the Triskèle, after it had lost one of its arms.   A design bearing a strong resemblance to the Triskèle is on the shield of *Gryx*, the legendary King of Sicily, as depicted on a vase in the Museum at Naples.   Experts have put its date at before 400 B.C.

A tolerably convincing proof that the ancients associated the Snake with Fire is furnished on Plate V, fig. 15.   It is an exact copy of a brooch found a few years ago, during the excavation of a Roman camp on the Saalburg, not far from Frankfort on the Main.   It has been placed in the Museum of the Kursaal at Homberg v.d. Hohe.   In this brooch, each of the three arms of the Triskèle or double Sun-Snake (as the late Prof. Kaṁer Herr Worsaae styled the Svastika of that type) is represented with a serpent's head.   Fig. 13 is a Svastika from the same collection enclosed in a rim of metal.   During the Bronze age, the duration of which the late Professor Dr Worsaae fixed at from about 500 B.C. to 100 A.D., the form of the Svastika received several modifications, amongst others it became what he styled the single S (*a*), the double S or double Sun snake (*b*), also the three-armed figure called the Triquetrum or the Triskèle.

(a)

(b)

There is even now, in our very midst, a phase of Sun and Fire symbolism which seems to have hitherto received but little attention—viz., the presence of such symbols in the crests or in the coats of arms of many of the oldest noble families and landed gentry of the British Isles. These appear in the greatest numbers in the armorial bearings of our Scottish families, and of those belonging to the northern counties of England, probably for the same reason that they are more numerous on objects which have been found in the northern portions of Scandinavia, *i.e.*, that the light and warmth of the sun were naturally prized in such districts, and they may also have survived there longer, since the isolated position of their inhabitants deprived them of much intercourse with the outer world.

We find at least three distinct forms of Sun and Fire symbolism in the crests and armorial bearings of many of our families.

(1.) The Sun in splendour.

(2.) Fire represented sometimes by a mountain in flames.

(3.) The Sun as a ring, or as a simple circle, the heraldic term for this latter type being *amulets* and *annulets*.

The following examples are some of the most typical of each kind.

Blount, *Bart.* This family is of French extraction,

formerly they were lords of Guisnes in France; their crest—
an armed foot in the Sun, and their motto—*Lux tua via mea.*

Blunt, *Bart.*   Probably originally the same family.
These latter have as their crest the Sun in glory, charged
in the centre with an eye issuing tears.   In the Earl of
Clancarty's arms (the Trenches came from Poitou in 1575)
on the first and third quarters is the Sun in splendour,
and in the centre an escutcheon with the coronet of a
Marquis of the Netherlands, charged with a wheel with
six spokes : as we have seen in Chapter III, the wheel
is still used in Denmark, Holland, and in parts of Germany,
as a preservative against fire.

Musgrave, *Bart.*, of Edenhall, has for his crest two arms
in armour embowed, and sustaining an annulet, so also has
Musgrave, *Bart.*, of Tourin, Co. Waterford, Ireland : their
arms are the same.

The rising Sun, and the Sun in his splendour is also
borne by the Marquis of Lothian, the Earl of Stamford
and Warrington, and by Lords Polwarth and Hammond ;
Lord Polwarth's crest is a Lady richly attired, holding a
Sun in her right hand, and a half moon in her left.   The
Sun also forms the crest of the Earl of Antrim, and of
Tyrwhitt, Fairbairn, and Nicholson, *Barts.* (where it is
placed between two stars of eight points), and of many
other families.

Fire symbols exist in connection with those of the Sun,
in the arms of Macleod of Lewis, whose crest is the Sun
in splendour ; in the first quarter of the arms is a mountain
in flames, in the second the three-legged Manx-man ; the
motto   belonging   to   this   latter   is   " Quocunque   jeceris

stabit "—" However you throw me I stand." This is true of the Svastika likewise.

The Earl of Cromartie bears this same symbol in his arms in the first and third quarters for Macleod, so also do the Dukes of Athole.

The Isle of Man was at one time owned by the Macleods; in 1405 it came into the possession of the Stanleys (afterwards Earls of Derby), and eventually, in 1735, devolved upon the ducal house of Athole, through the marriage of Amelia Anna Sophia, youngest daughter of the seventh Earl of Derby, by his wife Charlotte de la Tremouille (the Lady of Lathom), daughter of the Duc de Thouars in France, with John, second Earl, and first Marquis of Athole. On a seal in the possession of a member of that family is the motto *Luceo non uro* (I give light, but I do not burn). Beneath this is a Baron's coronet for the Barony of Strange, which came to the Dukes of Athole through the female line, and below this again, the Sun in glory. It is believed (but none are now living who know this for a fact) that this seal formerly belonged to Marjory, eldest daughter of James, sixteenth Lord Forbes, widow of John Lord Macleod, who died s. p. in 1789, and second wife of the fourth Duke of Athole. The Manx emblem correctly described, is " the three legs of a man armed proper, conjoined in the centre at the upper part of the thighs, placed in a triangle, garnished and spurred, *or*." We may add yet another variety of the Triskèle which forms the crest of the Tremaynes— a Cornish family—it consists of three *arms* with clenched fists placed in the same position—" conjoined at the shoulders, and flexed in triangles—*or*, fists proper." It is possible that this family may have adopted this symbol as a play upon their name, or what seems perhaps more likely, that the name was derived from the crest.   We have thus endeavoured to trace the outcome of the Trinacria of Sicily, and of the three-legged Manx-Man from the Scandinavian triskele of the Bronze Age (See Plate I, fig 12) and the Roman type of the same symbol with the serpents' heads.   A singular superstition exists still in some parts of England.   In Gloucestershire and in Here-fordshire it is a not uncommon circumstance to see on the external walls of some of the older houses one or two pieces of hoop iron of the forms (1) and sometimes as in (2).   It seems evident that they cannot render much, if any, support to the building, since they are bolted to it at one point only.   An interesting explanation regarding the virtue which the common people attach to these irons was given a few years ago by an old servant of our family, a Gloucester-shire man, who died at an advanced age: his years went with the century.   When asked the reason of their S form, he replied, " that the irons were made thus in order to protect the house from fire, as well as from falling down."   On being told this, a lady friend, who in her childhood resided in Camberwell, when it was not the populous suburb it has since become, said, " she well remembered one of their women servants giving the same reason for their presence on the house.   The late professor, Sir Charles Newton, in a lecture delivered in December 1893, on the monuments of Lycian art, alludes to an interesting series of Lycian silver coins, which he refers to the period between the conquest of Lycia under Cyrus and the overthrow of the Persian dynasty by Alexander. He says that these coins were struck by a number of autonomous cities, and are inscribed with their names in Lycian characters, also that they have on one side the curious symbol called the *triquetrum*, resembling the Manx three legs. Sir Charles was of opinion that "these coins belonged to a people whose original name was Tremilæ, a race belonging to the Aryan family, who were afterwards called Lycians. Another race, called the Solymi, were a Semitic people; they inhabited Lycia contemporaneously with the Tremilæ, but were driven back into the mountains on the east and north frontiers, and in the end the Tremilæ became mixed with the Greek settlers along the coast."

NOTE BY MAJOR R. C. TEMPLE.

[A good deal has been made by the English mythological school of writers of the fact that the Christian *Svastikas* point to the left, or westwards, whereas the Indian, including Buddhist and Jain *Svastikas*, point to the right, or eastwards. Letting alone that the right in India is southwards and never eastwards, the following observations on undoubted Buddhist *Svastikas* will probably go far to settle the theories built up on the pointing of the *cross fylfot*. In the *Inscriptions from the Cave Temples of Western India*, Bombay, 1881, are given a quantity of clearly Buddhist Square Pâli inscriptions from Kudâ, Kârlê, Śailarwâdi, Junnar, etc. Many of these contain *Svastikas* at the beginning and end. Kudâ No. 27 has (*a*) at the end ; but at the end of No. 29 is (*b*), which occurs again at the beginning and end of Junnar 30, at the beginning of Junnar 5, 20, 28, 32, and 34, and at the

(*a*)

(*b*)

end of Junnar 31, whilst (*a*) occurs at the beginning of Kudâ 30, and of Junnar 6 and 27, and at the end of 28.   The form (*c*) at the end of the Kolhâpur inscription, and (*b*) at the end of Kârlî No. 2.   In this last example, the thickening of the ends of the cross is probably due to the method of engraving.   It will be seen, therefore, that the pointing of the *Svastika* was not due, in Pâli inscriptions, to its position, nor was it in any way constant.]

ASIATIC SYMBOLISM.

Plate I.

SUN AND FIRE SYMBOLS FROM DENMARK, OF THE EARLIER BRONZE AGE.

OF THE LATER BRONZE AGE

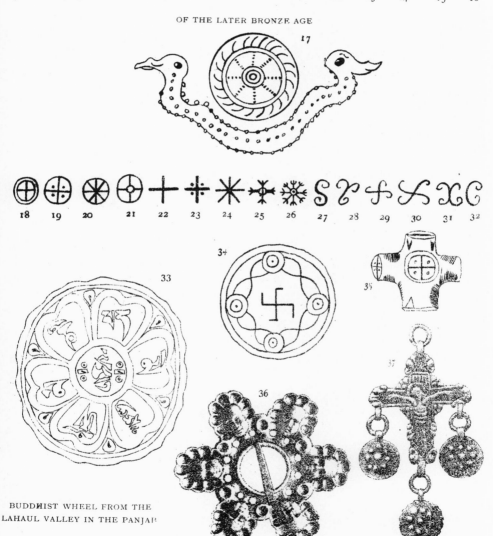

BUDDHIST WHEEL FROM THE
LAHAUL VALLEY IN THE PANJAB

WIZARD'S DRUM FROM LAPLAND.

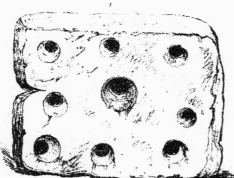

PIERRE BLANCHE AT KERUN ARRADON,
NEAR VANNES

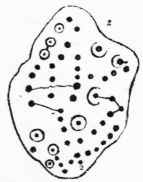

FROM A DOLMEN AT BAKER HILL,
ROSSHIRE, N.B.

MENHIR FROM BRITTANY.

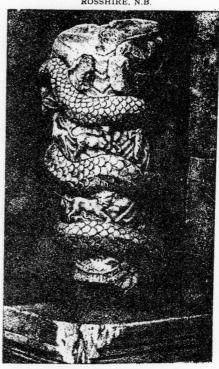

MITHRA, WITH SIGNS OF THE ZODIAC
FROM THE MUSEUM AT ARLES.

Plate 4.

STONE IN THE FOREST PARISH GUERNSEY

THREE BROTHERS OF GRUGITH
AT ST. KEVERNE, CORNWALL.

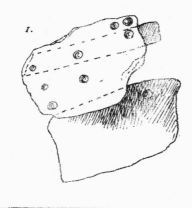

LA GARENNE ON L'ANCRESSE COMMON, GUERNSEY

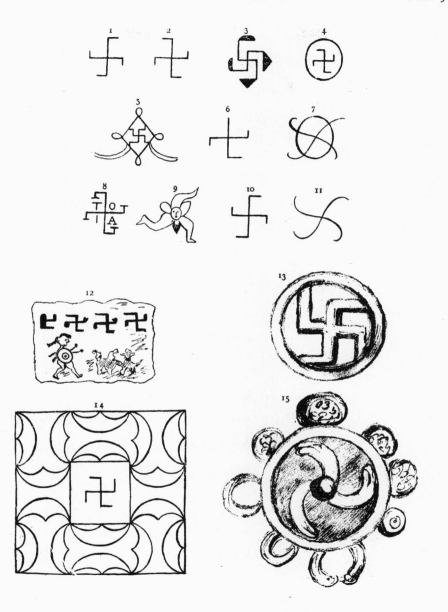

THE SVASTIKA.

ASIATIC SYMBOLISM.

SMALL ORNAMENTAL JAPANESE VASE.

BORDER OF
A CARPET FROM LEH.

ORNAMENT ON A
JAPANESE SPEAR,

CENTRAL MEDALLION OF A CARPET FROM LEH.

SHAFT OF THE SPEAR
SHOWING POSITION
OF THE ORNAMENT.

Plate 6.

Nos. 1, 2, 3 & 4.—MONOLITHS ON THE SUMMIT OF PANDAKOLI, IN KUMÂUN.
No. 5.—MONOLITHS IN TARTARY.   No. 6.—MONOLITH IN NAXOS.

Plate 8.

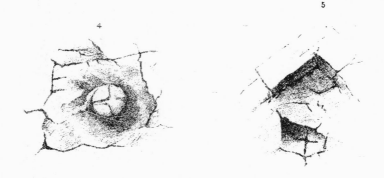

SCULPTURED STONES AND MONOLITHS IN THE ISLAND OF GUERNSEY

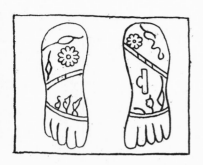

2

3

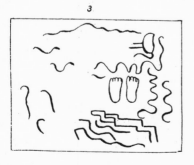

1. FROM BENARES.   2. FROM GOVARDHAN
3. FROM ARZON, MORBIHAN, BRITTANY.

4 TYPE OF MONOLITH COMMON IN SOUTHERN RUSSIA

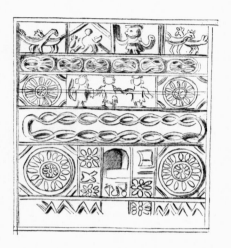

A STONE BY THE ROADSIDE NEAR SISSU IN LAHOUL.

LA VENUS DE QUINIPILY, NEAR BAUD MORBIHAN,
BRITTANY.

MONOLITH NEAR PONT L'ABBÉ, BRITTANY.

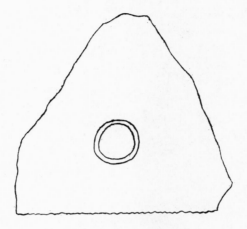

THE TOLVEN.
NEAR GWEEK, CONSTANTINE,
CORNWALL.

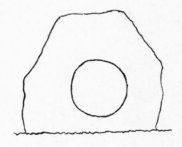

THE MEN-AN-TOL, MADRON, CORNWALL,
LOOKING S.W

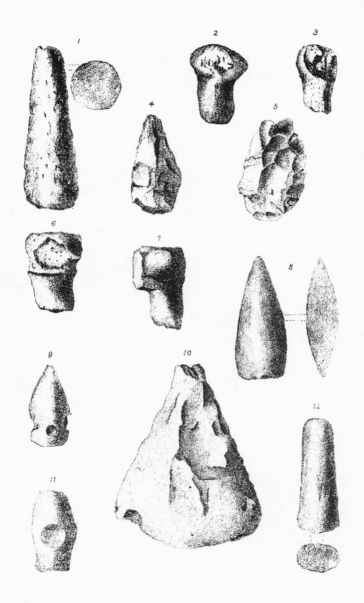

STONE CELTS FROM THE BÂNDÂ AND MIRZÂPUR DISTRICTS.

Plate 14.

STONE CELTS FROM GUERNSEY.

TATAR IDOL

FROM KANAUJ

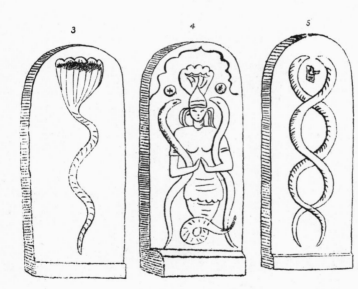

3, 4, 5. FROM MAISUR.

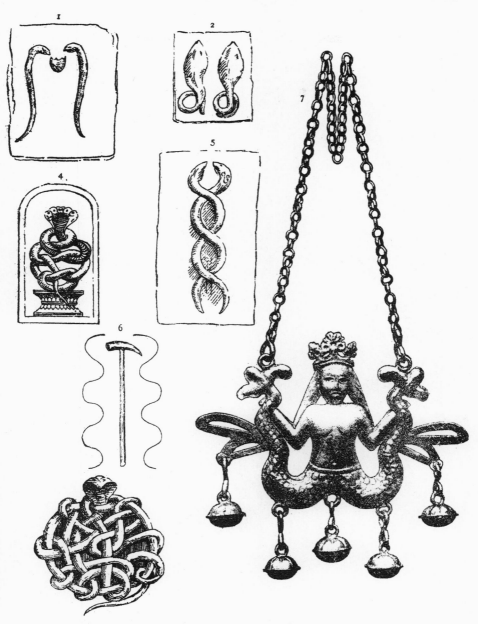

LA SIRENA.

VARIOUS FORMS OF A TALISMAN STILL IN USE AT NAPLES.

A BROOCH OF THE BRONZE AGE FROM NORWAY.

A BROOCH OF THE NORWEGIAN TYPE FROM A GRAVE
NEAR BREGENZ, IN SWITZERLAND.

Plate 19.

OLD AND NEW CHURCHES AT BORGUND—IN NORWAY.

NEPALI TEMPLE AT BANARAS.

PEASANT'S STORE-HOUSE AT BREDLAND THELMARKEN, NORWAY.

ASIATIC SYMBOLISM. *Plate 22.*

SCULPTURES FROM THE CLOISTERS OF TARRAGONA CATHEDRAL.

FROM THE BASE OF A PILLAR IN THE SOUTH WEST CORNER.

FROM THE CAPITAL OF A COLUMN.

FROM THE CAPITAL OF A COLUMN.

CHAPTER V

SOME CONNECTING LINKS BETWEEN THE TAU OF EGYPT, THE
CROSS AS A HEATHEN AND A CHRISTIAN SYMBOL, AND THE
HAMMER OF THE SCANDINAVIAN GOD THOR

IN his work on the Ancient Egyptians, Sir J. Gardner Wilkinson calls the *tau* "the sacred sign, or the sign of life."
"Its origin," he continues, "I cannot precisely determine,
but this curious fact is connected with it in later times—
that the early Christians of Egypt adopted it in lieu of the
Cross, which was afterwards substituted for it ; prefixing it
to inscriptions in the same manner as the Cross in later times,
and numerous inscriptions headed by the *tau* are preserved
to the present day in early Christian sepulchres at the great
Oasis." The coronation of the Egyptian kings was performed with great ceremony. They were anointed with oil
after they had been attired in rich robes ; a part of the same
ceremony was the blessing bestowed by the gods on the king
at the moment when he assumed the reins of government.
The gods laid their hands on him, and presented him
with the *tau* or symbol of life, which emblem, together with
the sceptre of purity, was usually placed in the hands of the
gods. The Egyptians constructed and accurately levelled
dykes and canals, in order that every cultivator might receive
the benefit of the inundations of the Nile. Its rise and fall
was exactly measured on Nilometers, by particular persons
appointed to that office, in order to note its daily change ;

63

and on their reports depended the time for opening the canals.   These were closed until the river rose to a fixed height, when they were opened by cutting away the dam of earth which separated them from the Nile.

It would seem not improbable that the gift of the *tau* or *crux ansata*—as it has been called—to the Sovereign at his Coronation may have been intended to signify the bestowal on him by the gods of a typical key of the waters of the Nile, *i.e.*, that it was a token of supreme power ; thus it would not unnaturally be regarded as a sign of life, for without it the land could not yield its increase.   In like manner, the *tau* or cross may have come to be worshipped as the symbol of light and generation, or feared as an image of decay or death.   At first sight it is not very apparent why the *scarab*—the beetle should have been sacred to the Egyptians ; but if we examine one of these insects, we shall find that the sutures down the back and across the thorax form a **T**.   Curiously enough, the peasantry in some parts of England call this insect the *tor* or *dor* beetle.   The carpet alluded to in Chapter IV. as being in the writer's possession, and coming from Khotan in Yarkand, is bordered with *Svastikas* of the Chinese form.   It is worthy of remark that when, as in this instance, a Chinese *Svastika* is placed in a square (as in the enclosed sketch), the intervening spaces form **T**'s or *taus*.   Certain Hindû ascetics in India,

 who are in the habit of sitting for days and nights together in a Buddha-like attitude on the ground, use a kind of crutched cross in the form of a *tau* on which to rest their arms.

The remarkable designs figured below are taken from the Habbakhorten Mosque

in Kashmir, situated about a couple of miles higher up the
river than the European quarter of Śrînagar. It is most
singular to find here such symbols as the Cross and the
Svastika on a Muhammedan building. The boat people say
it was erected in the time of the Emperor Jahângir, who
reigned from 1605 to 1628.

In 1896, Dr Arthur Neve, a medical missionary in
Śrînagar, the capital of Kashmir, made a short summer tour
to Chilas, and some of the remote parts of the Kohistân, west
of Kashmir. On his return he gave me sketches he had made
of some stone and wooden grave monuments in the Muhammedan cemeteries of those districts. He very frequently
observed, sculptured on the upper part of these stones or
wooden posts, what was evidently intended to represent a
head of the Markhor or wild sheep ; occasionally two such
were placed back to back :—Markhor horns are still
put on graves. Below the head is a double circle
having a cross in the centre, the cross being carved
in high relief or often perforated. In a note attached
to the drawings, Dr Neve states that the effigy of the Markhor
head is abundant on the graves of poor people, and that the
cross is only found on these monuments in Upper Khâgan

and Khel.   He adds, that in Lower Khâgan it is usually
modified into a hexagonal or octagonal ornament, but in
these cases it is never carved in such relief or perforated.

The presence of the Cross, the *Svastika*, and other
symbols on a Muhammedan building, and of an animal's
head and a Cross on Muhammedan graves, is most remarkable, since this faith, as a rule, does not allow of symbolism
of any kind, still less of the effigy of any living thing.

Moor, the author of the *Hindû Pantheon* in his *Oriental
Fragments*, p. 477, states that the Greek *tau* or T is supposed
to have been the sign which in later days distinguished the
names of the living after a battle, etc.—from the dead,
the names of these latter being marked with a Θ, a letter
indicating "dead."   Thus the *tau* was then held to be the
symbol of life.   On page 76 of this work he speaks of a
seal in his possession dug up a few years previously near
his house in Suffolk.   He conceives this object to have
some reference to Hindûism, though unconsciously on the
part of the designer.   "This," he adds, "is the original seal
of the great Lazar house of Burton in Leicestershire."
Its form is the lozenge or doubled cone, and in the centre
is a figure which he takes to be either St Augustine or
St Lazarus.   If we look into the matter we can see what
he means by this seal having some reference to Hindûism;
we can trace on the badges and medals of some of our
Ecclesiastical Guilds and Societies their possible outcome
from the two principal emblems of Śiva.   With us now
these symbols have come to be called the *Vesica Piscis*
and the Cross, but if we regard them in their original
symbolic aspect, we can hardly fail to see their Hindû

origin. At the present day the Hindûs deem it a very meritorious act to plant a grove of trees of any species to enable the wayfarer to obtain shade and rest, more especially so when composed of Mango trees, to refresh him with their fruit; likewise to cause a tank to be excavated for the public benefit. The water of the tank, however, is not considered by them to be pure or wholesome until it has been in a manner consecrated by having a long pole driven down in its centre: this they style marrying the tank.

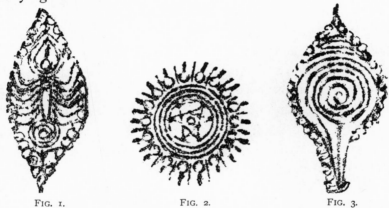

FIG. 1.   FIG. 2.   FIG. 3.

Some of the seals used by the Vaishnava sect to impress upon deeds, and also on certain occasions to stamp upon their persons, have the form of the *Vesica*. Fig. 1, the Scorpion, is very typical. On fig. 2 is the six-pointed star or Solomon's seal, as it is styled; and on fig. 3 is a representation of the *Śankh* or Conch shell, which, when bored at one end, is used by them to call their votaries to worship. These are figured above; they are very interesting in the present connection.

The *tau*, as we shall proceed to show, is a very wide-spread emblem.

In 1886, at a meeting of the British Association, Mr G. Halliburton read a paper containing notes on a cross on the badge of a medicine-man of the Queen Charlotte Isles. " This symbol," he said, "was used by these people on large sheets of copper, to which they attached a high value, and each of which they called a *tau*. Their medicine-men sometimes have the *tau* impressed on their foreheads. The ancients used to mark the captives who were to be saved with a *tau* or cross."

" Figures of the *tau*," says Jomard, "are numerous in the buildings, bas-reliefs, and even in the form of the lights of the ancient city of Palenque in Central America, although," he adds, "it is impossible to form an opinion upon them in our present state of knowledge."

Again, Captain Bourke, U.S.A., in his work on the Moquis of Arizona, says: "Preparatory to taking part in the snake dance, old and young of both sexes put on curious head-dresses of boards, painted green or sky blue, with tips of red or yellow, in which were incisions in the shape of the crescent, the cross, or the letter T.

The order of St Antony of Ethiopia, one of the earliest orders of foreign knighthood, is recorded to have been founded by Prester John, the Christian Emperor in Africa, circa A.D. 370. He formed certain monks, who had led austere lives in the desert, into a religious .order of knighthood. Its members wore a black habit, and had for their ensign a blue cross edged with gold in the form of the letter T.

A *tau*, with a human head in place of the *ansa* or handle,
has been found depicted on the wall of a house in the
ruined city of Pompeii, in juxtaposition with the Phallus or
Lingam.

The Friars of the order of St Antony of Vienne, in
Dauphiné, who followed the rule of St Augustine, wore a
black habit, with the letter T in blue on their breasts. This
order was instituted about 1095 by a nobleman near Vienne
named Gaston and his son Girond, in consequence of a
pestilential erysipelas distemper called the Sacred Fire,
which raged there in 1089 and the following years. At
length it pleased God to grant many miraculous cures of
this dreadful distemper to those who implored his mercy
through the intercessions of St Antony.

The Friars of this order came to England, temp. Henry
III. About the year 1249, the parish of All Saint's, Hereford,
a rectory anciently in the gift of the Crown, together with
the Churches or Chapels of St Martin's and St Peter's
Bullinghope annexed, were given to the Hospital of St
Antony in London. This order would appear to have
formed, about that date, a small society in Hereford, in order
to superintend their property, of which the donation was
confirmed in 1294 (22nd Edw. I.). According to the *Ency.
Brit.*, there was also an order of the Knights of St Antony
instituted in 1382 by Albert Duke of Bavaria, against the
Turks. They wore a collar of gold, from which hung a
stick, cut like a *crutch*."

The cross was also widely known as a pre-Christian
symbol. The Spaniards, when they went to South America,
found the cross in some of the heathen temples there ; they

are said to have imagined at first that St Thomas had
penetrated thither as well as to India as a missionary, until
they heard of the human sacrifices which were practised in
connection with it, when they concluded it was the work
of the evil one—being unaware that the *Svastika* (a form
of the cross) had existed in Asia before European history
began.   In Mexico they are said to have been much struck
with the stone crosses, which they found on the coast and
in the interior of the country, which were considered objects
of veneration and worship.   To the Mexicans the cross was
a symbol of rain, and of the fertilising element—or rather of
the four winds, the bearers of rain.   It would appear that
the cross had also another signification for them, since
near the spot where the city of Vera Cruz was afterwards
built, there was a marble cross surmounted by a golden
crown.   In reply to the enquiries of the Spanish ecclesiastics,
the natives said, "that one more glorious than the Sun had
died upon the Cross."

The cross was considered a rain symbol by the Mexicans,
and their name for it, *Tomaquahuitl,* or the tree of life, would
seem to combine the two ideas of fertility conferred by the
possession of the *tau* or cross, and salvation through the
cross or tree of life.

It is only within the last few years that the cross has been
known to have existed among the prehistoric peoples of North
America as well as among some of its present Indian tribes,
who use it both as a Sun and a weather-symbol.   The so-
called Mound-builders of St Louis, U.S.A., were also familiar
with the cross.   In a narrow valley near the little town of
Tarlton, in Ohio, there is a remarkable earthwork in the

form of a Greek cross ✚. It is raised about three feet above the adjacent surface : round it is a shallow ditch exactly corresponding to its outline. Amongst other relics which have been found on opening some of these mounds—are inscribed shells or shell gorgets, as they have been styled, on the supposition that they were, most probably, neck or throat ornaments. One of the most remarkable is the so-called bird gorget, in the centre of which is a cross of the Greek type, placed within a circle, around which is a star of eight points : an apparent combination of the Cross and the Sun. Opposite the four arms of the cross are rudely drawn birds' heads. Some of these ornaments have been styled spider gorgets— the centre of the disk having a figure of this insect. On some of the latter is a Greek cross, a wheel cross, or a figure of the cross only—without any other symbol, also a plain cross on a disk of copper, and a singular form of the *Svastika*, similar to one which exists as a mason's mark on the lower platform of the Tâj Mahâl at Agra.

The aboriginal tribes of North America were also in the habit of using astronomical symbols and signs to express astronomical events. Many of these signs were common to, and could therefore be understood by, different tribes, and thus served as mediums of intercommunication when difference of language was a bar to nearer intercourse.

Such symbols were mainly the expression of *religious thought*, whilst their sign language treated of the common affairs of life. It would appear that certain Indian tribes had a common mythology, and a common astronomy; thus such symbols would be easily understood by all.

The Black-foot Indians are in the habit of arranging

boulders in the form of a cross.   According to them, stones thus arranged symbolise the "Old man in the Sun, who rules the Winds:" they mark his resting places, and the limbs of the cross represent his body and arms.   Among the Delawares the rain makers draw upon the ground a figure of the Cross, and cry aloud to the Spirit of the rains.

It is, and probably will remain, a mystery to us how and whence the cross reached America; from its presence on the objects found within the mounds of St Louis, the presumption is that this symbol was used by prehistoric races of whom we have absolutely no knowledge, except from their primitive monuments and relics.

We will now turn to Scandinavian symbolism, bearing in mind that Scandinavia did not become Christian till the beginning of the eleventh century; the people seem to have adopted the Latin form of the cross, but we are brought into close contact also with Sun and Moon and Fire-worship, since, for a time at least, they still retained their Sun symbolism in connection with their new faith, as is evidenced by a small crucifix with pendant Sun symbols in the writer's possession (Plate I, fig. 37). Another specimen, not figured in this work, shows that, later on, small pendants in the form of the Latin cross were sub-stituted for the Sun emblems attached to the arms and the base of the earlier example.   In these countries we also meet with the *tau* of Egypt and the *Svastika* or Hindû and Buddhist form of the cross.   The *Svastika* was the emblem of Thor, the chief god of their mythology—their god of the air, of thunder and lightning as well as of Fire;

he was the Zeus of the Greeks and the Jove of the Romans. In order to find the thunder emblem we will now carry our readers back with us to the mythology and symbolism of 2500 years ago. The author possesses a so-called Babylonian cylinder on which is represented the god Rimmon, the god of the air; he holds a thunderbolt in his right hand. This figure is most interesting in connection with Bible history (2 Kings v. 18). This same symbol exists down to our own times. The Romans placed a similar weapon in the hand of Jove. It serves also to show that the *Svastika*, the special emblem of Thor, the thunder god of Scandinavia, was accepted as one of the powers of the air. An object of precisely the same form as the thunderbolt of Rimmon is now used in Tibet (and we believe in some parts of India also) as a powerful weapon against evil spirits, and also as a curative agent in cases of sickness. It is styled a *Vajra*, in Tibetan a r*Do-rje* or thunderbolt. The *Phûr-pa*, or Nail, is

DO-RJE OR VAJRA.

with these peoples another important weapon of the same character; it is likewise of brass, dagger shaped, and surmounted by representations of the heads of the three most powerful *Drag-gsheds* (tutelary deities or good genii); a r*Do-rje* or thunderbolt forms the handle part. Below this is the head of *Tamdin*, another Drag-gshed, noted for his power; the lower end is triangular, and sharp pointed. In cases of illness a Lama (or Buddhist monk) goes round the house turning the point of the *Phûr-bu* or *Phûr-pa* in all directions, and uttering magical spells.

To return, however, to Thor who, as stated above, was the chief god in Scandinavian mythology. He is fabled to have waged war with giants, and to have killed them with his hammer or mallet, called Mjolmir (another cross-like symbol), his great weapon of destruction : to it was ascribed the marvellous property of always returning to its owner after having been launched upon its mission.

Numberless realistic as well as conventional forms of the hammer of Thor are exhibited in the Historical Museum at Stockholm.   Many of these little ornaments from their shape seem to establish a link between the *tau* and the more usual forms of the cross.   One such is a perfect Egyptian *tau*, wanting only the *ansa* or handle at the upper end ; it has Sun symbols attached to the arms and base.   All are, for the most part, of silver or silver gilt, some are wrought with elaborate designs in filigree ; and in some cases the chain by which they were suspended was found with them.   One such chain is specially interesting : its make is precisely the same as the Trichinopoly chains of Southern India,

As we have stated above, Thor, being regarded as the god of Fire (as is shown by his *Svastika* emblem), he was naturally held to be the god of the domestic hearth. His hammer was also looked upon as an instrument of *possession*.

When a bride entered her new home one of Thor's hammers was thrown into her lap.   Thursday (Thor's-day) is still deemed in Scandinavia an auspicious day for marrying ; and a man when buying a piece of land takes possession of it by throwing a hammer upon it.

This same idea enters into Indian mythology also.   Vishnu, in one of his Avatârs or successive incarnations, is fabled to have taken possession of a considerable extent of land in the kingdom of Travancore by throwing his battle-axe on it.[1]

The Maoris or aborigines of New Zealand also attach the same meaning to their stone celts and hammers ; most unwillingly, if ever, will they sell or give one of their stone implements to a European—holding that by so doing they would lose their rights of proprietorship on the soil.

A very few years ago great joy arose in a certain district in that country on the accidental discovery of a very sacred stone axe, which was known to have been secretly buried long long before by one of their ancestors. The story of its discovery runs thus :[2] " A young married woman had gone into the forest, December 10th, 1887, with her husband and some others to collect mushrooms. She wandered away from her companions, when on putting down her hand to gather some growing at the foot of a tree, she saw a sudden bright light, and following this with her eyes, she perceived an axe : she gave a loud cry which attracted her husband to the spot, and then ran away. At this moment there was a tremendous thunderclap, very vivid lightning, and a violent hailstorm burst. The following day a large company of people, headed by two priests, who recited charms and incantations, went in procession to the spot, carrying branches of foliage in their hands. They had scarcely arrived at the place when they heard successive claps of thunder, accompanied with lightning. Soon a

[1] It is a well-known fact that the land has been gradually rising on that part of the coast ; Cranganore, once a flourishing seaport, has long been disused from this cause ; and another, Alleppi, within the memory of man, is rapidly sharing a similar fate.

[2] Taken from a native journal called the *Korimoko*, published in Maori, and translated into English by Mr Edmund Tregear of Wellington, New Zealand.

thick fog came on, and it became as dark as night. The Tohunga (priests) by their incantations arrested the thunder and dispersed the darkness."

This legend would seem to show that these people, like the Scandinavians, associated thunder—one of the attributes of Thor—with the hammer or axe which was his weapon. With us, too, the notion of possession is attached to the hammer, thus connecting our own times with the beliefs and mythology of ancient and savage peoples; for the mallet or hammer has its use in Masonic ritual as a symbol of authority, and the auctioneer with a tap of his hammer confers the possession of an article on the highest bidder.

Have the peoples of Europe and the Indians retained these ideas since the time when their ancestors used only stone implements? The Maoris, not having iron tools until the advent of the white man, may be said to be even now only partially emerged from the Stone Age.

NOTE.—For further illustrations connected with the Tau and the Cross, reference may be made to Wilkinson's *Egyptians*, vol. i., pp. 365, 376 ; vol. ii., p. 283 ; vol. v., pp. 283, 284 ; and vol. vi., 'Khem' ; Landseer's *Sabean Researches*, p. 361 ; Warburton's *Crescent and Cross*, vol. ii., p. 314 ; King's *Gnostics*, p. 135 ; or Hislop's *Two Babylons*, 4th ed., pp. 322 *ff*.

CHAPTER VI

SACRED STONES

IN the Bible the prophet Isaiah condemns the stone worship of his day in the following words: " Slaying the children in the valleys under the clifts of the rocks? Among the smooth stones of the stream is thy portion: they, they are thy lot: even to them thou hast poured a drink offering, thou hast offered a meat offering. Should I receive comfort in these? "

In India, at the present day, both the Śaiva and the Vaishnava sects of Hindûs have their sacred stones. The *lingas* of the Śaivas exist in all their temples, while the Vaishnavas have their *śâlagrâmas*.

The Vaishnavas as well as the modern Jainas reverence the impression on stone of the soles of two feet,—a Vaishnava temple at Gayâ being called Bishn-pad, or Vishnu's foot.[1] Plate IX, fig. 1, is a representation of this emblem from the Râjâ of Nâgpur's palace at Benares. Fig. 2 is a mosaic pavement in the centre of the floor of the Chhatrî or cenotaph at Govardhan, erected to the memory of a former Mahârâjâ of Bharatpur. This symbol is not unknown in Europe ; it forms a portion of the ornamentation on one of the large stones within a dolmen at Arzon in the Morbihan, South

[1] Of this symbol the late Kamer Herr Dr Worsaae said : " It frequently occurs on rock cuttings in Bohuslehn, in the south of Sweden (the ancient Scania), and it has been considered a sacred sign over the whole earth, being in India an emblem of Buddha and of Vishnu."

Brittany (see Plate IX, fig. 3).   In the Island of Guernsey, on the Roquaine road, and not far from L'Erée, is a field in which is a rocky mound.   On the surface of the stone, which is of granite, are two depressed traces of foot-marks in opposite directions.   The depressions appear to be due to disintegration of the granite block, but so plainly do they resemble the impressions of two human feet, that one is forced to believe their present form was at some remote period greatly assisted by some rude sculptor's chisel.

An incident which happened to the writer when in Benares seems to throw some light upon the signification of this symbol in modern India.   One day, when wandering in the outskirts of the native city, the attention of some of the party was attracted to a temple which, though handsome, on closer examination proved to be an insignificant one ; but near it were two tombs : on the larger one was a *linga* and trident in bas-relief ; between these was the impression of the soles of two feet : the smaller tomb had only the two feet upon it.   Whilst wondering what could be the meaning of those symbols in such a position, a middle-aged native woman approached, and on being asked about these tombs, said : " The largest one is my father's tomb, the other is the tomb of my mother ; they were both Gosains, and so am I."   On being questioned still further, she added : " We use the signs of the feet to express worshipping at our parents' feet—*i.e.*, being their disciples."   It is well known that the Gosains bury their dead, contrary to the usual Hindû practice of cremation.

The worship of Śaiva stones undoubtedly prevailed in Kashmir at one period.   At a place called Pandrethan, rather less than two miles from the European quarter of

Śrînagar, a group of so-called Śaiva stones of enormous size existed a few years ago. In 1876 some were upright in their original position, and one or more, still perfect, were prostrate on the ground. In 1892 only a fragment of one of these ancient relics remained ; from the appearance it presented the rest of these stones must have been chipped away piecemeal, to be used most probably as triturators for red pepper or curry stuffs.

Baron von Hügel, in his *Travels in Kashmir and the Panjâb*, relates that he had found many such stones near the sacred spring at Islâmâbâd. Similar stones have also been found in places where Buddhism is known to have existed. It seems not improbable that these may be the relics of a still older form of religion than that of Buddha. Stones of this kind have also been found amongst the ruins of the old town of Valabhi in Kâthiâwâd ; the writer has, however, never met with them in Ladakh (Western Tibet), in the Himâlayan valleys of Spiti and Lahûl, in the upper part of the Satlaj valley, or in Ceylon, in all of which Buddhism now prevails to a greater or less extent.

On Plate IXA, is figured a remarkable piece of sculpture from the Lahaul valley ; it stands by the roadside between Sissu and Gondla. The drawing was taken on the spot in 1878, when we were on a marching tour : so far as we re-member, this stone is about five feet in height and rather less in breadth. The execution is rude, and the subject seems obscure. The figures wear the dress common to those regions ; the geometric designs, however, seem to belong to a more advanced style of art than we should have credited these people with.

Madden, in his account of the Tarâï and Kumâon, says : " A little below the point of the junction of the Gaulâ and the Baliyâ, at a holy spot called Maipûr or Mayâpûr, is the *Chitra Śilâ* or mottled stone—a large rounded boulder of quartz conglomerate—reposing in a deep cleft in the sandstone, which forms the right bank of the Gaulâ. It is sacred to Devî and Mahâdeo (*i.e.*, Śiva), and is greatly venerated."

In the Central Provinces the Gonds, generally held to be an aboriginal race, and who there sunk very low in the social scale, are still in the habit of choosing a rough stone of an oblong shape, which they daub over with a red pigment, set up under a pipal tree (*ficus religiosa*) and perform *pûjâ* (worship) to it. This consists in pouring oblations of milk over it, and making offerings of flowers, etc.[1] As an instance of the transfer of this custom to orthodox Vaishṇavism, when at Gayâ we saw a pilgrim place a small box of lucifer matches on a tray together with other offerings, and deposit them in the innermost shrine on the impression of the feet of Vishṇu.

The custom of making offerings and libations is not yet extinct in Europe. At the Point de Jerbourg, the most south-easterly promontory of the Island of Guernsey, is a tall rock, which, when viewed from a particular point, is said to bear some resemblance to a cowled monk. This rock is called by the country people " Le petit bon homme Andrelot." The fishermen when passing it take off their hats, and make a libation to it of any liquor which they may happen to have on board and throw some old clothes to it.

[1] This custom is by no means confined to the Gonds or to the Central Provinces.

In the book of the Wisdom of Solomon in the Apocrypha there is a passage which shows that a similar form of worship to that just noticed was practised in those times. It runs thus: " Miserable are they, and in dead things, is their hope, who called them gods which are the work of men's hands : gold and silver to show art in and resemblances of beasts or a stone good for nothing, the work of an ancient hand, and fashioned it to the image of a man, or made it like some vile beast, *laying it over with vermilion and with paint, colouring it red*, and covering every spot therein; then maketh he a prayer for his goods, for his wife and children, and is not ashamed to speak to that which hath no life. For health he calleth upon that which is weak ; for life, prayeth he to that which is dead ; for aid, humbly beseecheth that which hath least means to help, and for a good journey, he asketh of that which cannot set a foot forward."

Prior to the reformation of their faith by Muhammad, the ancient Arabs paid particular reverence to a stone called Al-Lât. In Musalmân books there are two stones called Al-Lât—viz., the pre-Islamite goddess Al-Lât worshipped as an idol, and the idol at Somnâth destroyed by Mahmûd of Ghazni in 1024 A.D. The form of this latter was conical ; it was the same as the *linga* worshipped everywhere in India as the emblem of Śiva. Muhammedan writers call it Lât and El Lât ; it has often been confounded with the ancient Arabian goddess the *real* Al-Lât. There is, however, no reason to suppose that this latter had the form of a *linga*.

In Rome, as well as in Greece and Etruria, it was only after the lapse of several centuries that art ventured to represent the gods under the human form. On this account the earlier inhabitants were accustomed to offer sacrifices to the trunks of trees, or to dark coloured stones, a habit which, according. to some passages in their poets, survived for a long time among the lower classes.   Indeed, from what we learn from Varro, for more than 170 years the Romans rendered worship to their gods without having any representations of them whatever; and Plutarch relates the story that when Numa regulated the ceremonies to be observed by the Romans, he forbade any objects of a definite form being exposed to public veneration.

It is the opinion of certain learned men, that such must have been introduced in the reign of the elder Tarquinius, who was an Etruscan.   This leads us to conjecture that he may have brought the system of image worship with him from his own country.

It would appear that stone worship was not unknown in Europe and in England even as late as the eleventh century.   Theodore, Archbishop of Canterbury, in the seventh century; the Saxon King Edgar in the tenth; and Canute, the Dane, in the eleventh, all forbade the worship of stone monuments, etc., of the remote ages.   At a Council held at Tours in the sixth century it was resolved that the Church doors should be closed against those who worshipped certain upright stones.

Mr Waring, in his *Stone Monuments and Tumuli*, says that he remembers having seen an Anglo-Saxon law to the effect that whosoever wished to preserve such stones might do so on payment of a fine to the Church.   A stone of this sort is possibly indicated in the *Edda*, the most ancient book of Scandinavia, where mention is made of an oath taken near the Sacred White Stone.   Mons. Holmböe, in his little work, *Buddhism en Norvège*, published in 1857, after speaking of sacred stones as known in Kashmir and India, goes on to say :—" It is most singular to find traces of the same customs in Norway.   The museum at Bergen possesses three stones of a greyish white marble.   One was brought from a large *Haug* (or tumulus) on a farm called Glein, in the island of Daumöe, off the coast of Heligoland.   This stone is like those from Balabhipura, in Sorath " (Valabhî in Kâthiâwâd), " three feet high, and nineteen inches in diameter.   Both tumulus and stone were formerly held sacred.   The two others were not found in tumuli, but such was probably their original position." [1] Another Norwegian antiquarian, Mons. Liligren, relates that in the year 1817, in a field in the parish of Sparhoe, in the diocese of Trondhjem, a stone of precisely the same form was discovered, and another in Vestmanland, in Sweden, and he gives it as his opinion that they had been worshipped as gods.   Mr Christie also speaks of a similar stone, " which tradition says existed formerly near the town of Tromsöe, in Finmark, and was worshipped by the Laplanders, and that the Bishop in consequence had it removed and thrown into the river."   Mr Christie says also that he himself had seen " on the farm called Opsanger, in the parish of Quindherred, in the diocese of Bergen, on the summit of a large tumulus, a stone of the same kind."   Stones of this form, when found in Norway, are supposed to date from the Iron Age in Scandinavia.   In another place Mons. Holmböe says : " According to the ancient laws of Scandinavia, put

[1] Since this was written at least ten more such stones have been found in Norway.

forth in the first century, after the introduction of Christianity there, it is especially forbidden to worship stones." He also adds : " We will now pass on to another form, which appears also to have been considered sacred. These are stones of a spheroidal or ovoid form, which have been found in certain tumuli. One such stone, nine inches in length and seven in circumference, was found within the cell of a tumulus not far from the town of Flekkefjord, in Norway. He then goes on to say : " The Museum at Bergen possesses two stones, which in size and colour exactly resemble hen's eggs ; they are made of some white stone, probably marble, and were found in a tumulus in the district of Sandfjord, in the diocese of Bergen. The proprietor of the land told me that he found them in the cell in the centre of the tumulus." He next proceeds to enumerate several places where spherical or oval stones of the same description have been found in Norway, and also in Denmark, in Livonia, and in the north of Germany. Now, in one part of the bazar of the native city at Benares, hundreds of spherical or oval stones are exhibited for sale. They are for the most part of the size and form of a common hen's egg. Possibly they are used in private worship. It is well known to all who have ever been in India that no Hindû, except a *Pariah* (or outcaste), will eat a hen's egg or even keep fowls.

The Śaiva sect is said to regard the hen's egg [1] as a symbol of creation ; the bull also was an emblem used in the same connection ; it is one of the emblems of Śiva. The figure of a bull is invariably placed in the porch or within the precincts of temples dedicated to that god.

[1] A Brahman lady from Bengal recently told the writer that they made an exception in favour of ducks' eggs ; these they may partake of.

A most remarkable symbolic link would seem to exist between the Hindû and the Japanese religion as regards the egg and the bull. At Miaco, in Japan, there is a pagoda in honour of a bull; the animal is represented standing on a broad square altar of massive gold, a rich collar is round its neck, but the object which principally attracts attention is an egg, which it holds between its fore feet, and is in the act of striking with its horns. The egg represents chaos, and, according to the legend, the entire world during the time of chaos was enclosed in that egg, which floated upon the surface of the waters. The Moon, by its influence and the power of its light, drew up earthy matter from the bottom of the waters, which became hard rock, on which the egg rested. The bull, finding this egg, broke it with its horns, and from the shell burst forth the world; the breath of the bull produced man. Such is the explanation of these objects as given by Japanese learned men.

Spherical stones again, according to Mr Masson, have been found in Afghanistan and other places also. They have invariably been found in the centre of monuments, as described above, which position, Mr Masson is of opinion, was given to them with some special object.

Such stones take yet another form in Scandinavia. Of these, three or four specimens exist in the Museum of Antiquities at Stockholm. It seems, however, an open question whether they can be considered Śaiva stones. They perfectly correspond with a description given by Mons. Liligren of certain stones in a passage he quotes from a manuscript by M. Schöning, Bishop of Trondhjem, relating to a custom which existed in Norway at the end of the eighteenth century.   M. Schöning says : "At the farm of Qualset, in the Telemarken district, two stones were still preserved at the end of the last century of the form of loaves of common rye bread—that is to say, round, and convex on their upper side.   These stones were so much esteemed that they were placed upon seats of honour and *bathed regularly with milk and butter, and at Christmas watered with fresh beer.*"[1]   There are yet other kinds of sacred stones, some of which are still in use in India, and of which examples still exist in Europe—viz., stone circles, monoliths, and stone implements.

In one of Mr H. Rivett-Carnac's papers on the rock sculptures and monoliths of Kumâon, he mentions a stone circle on the summit of Pandakoli (a mountain rising to the height of 8000 feet above the sea) within which four monoliths are standing.   This monument consists of an outer and an inner circle of stones.   The outer circle, sixteen feet in diameter, is composed of rough stones, piled one upon the other, with larger stones at the entrance.   The inner circle, eight feet in diameter, is made partly of large stones about three and a half feet in height, and partly of smaller ones. The entrance is to the south.

When describing the four monoliths on Pandakoli (see Plate VII, figs. 1, 2, 3, 4) Mr Rivett-Carnac says : "No priest lives on the hill; it is too cold, jungly, and inaccessible for a lengthened sojourn, but I learn that a fair is held there in the spring, when many pilgrims visit it, chiefly childless women."   He adds: "Fig. 1 has a mark upon it which was

---

[1] Libations of milk and of water, and oblations of flowers, are daily offered to Śiva, in Hindû worship, as well as to other gods.

perhaps intended for the Moon ; on fig. 3 is what looks like a Sun. Fig. 2 is a monolith of the same nature, from the summit of that mountain. Fig. 4 is another stone from Chandeswar in the same district." The English stone circles of Stonehenge and Avebury, in Wilts, are well known. Similar monuments exist also in the Channel Islands, in Guernsey, and on the island of Herm. Fig. 5 is a stone from Tartary, given both in front and in side face. Fig. 6 is from the island of Naxos in Greece. The two latter bear a strange resemblance to each other, but, we would remark, it is probably a still more singular circumstance to find the same types of stones existing in Europe, and still used as places of pilgrimage by women—the *menhir* of Kergloas in Brittany for example. On Plate X is represented a statue, locally known as the Venus de Quinipily, taken from a sketch made by a friend some years ago. It is situated near Baud, Morbihan, Brittany. Black, in his *Guide to Brittany,* gives the following description of it : " It is a nude, rudely formed stone statue, about eight feet high, standing against a slab. The thighs are disproportionately thin. Round the waist of the statue is a narrow girdle, the ends of which fall down in front ; the hands are crossed over the body. It stands on a pedestal nine feet high, rising from the front of a terrace over a dilapidated fountain. From the flatness of the features some have supposed it to have an Egyptian origin, but the probability is, that it does not date later than the sixteenth century, when it was the object of impure rites among the Bretons."

Near St Renan, and about twelve miles from Brest, is a monolith called the *menhir* of Kergloas, said to be the finest of its kind in Brittany.   It is a quadrangular stone of brownish granite, nineteen feet in circumference, and thirty-nine feet in height above ground; it tapers slightly towards the top.   On its eastern and western sides, at a height of about four feet from the ground, is a circular protuberance or boss; at that level the stone would be four feet thick in the centre and two feet at each side.   On and around the two bosses the stone has an almost polished appearance, whereas the rest is covered with a short and very fine species of lichen, caused probably by the action of the winds from the Atlantic.   Female pilgrims are said to visit this *menhir* at the present day.   Not improbably a habit of rubbing the lower part of this monolith may have contributed to produce the peculiar appearance of that portion.   It is worthy of notice that the Eastern boss seems to have been the most favoured in this respect.

On very good authority the writer learnt, a few years ago, that certain mysterious rites *are still* practised by childless women in some parts of Brittany.   An artist, staying in a small town on the north coast, went out one moonlight night to make a sketch of a Dolmen or ancient stone monument.   He presently heard some people approaching, and having been told that it was dangerous to be supposed to be watching them at such times, he retired into the shadow, and saw two women come near this stone, and proceed to move round and round it. After a time they departed, and he returned to his hotel. On his return he saw a carriage being taken back into the stable-yard, and asked the coachman where he had been.   The man was surly at first, but when a five-franc

piece was put into his hand, he informed the artist that
he had driven two women to the *menhir*, one of whom
was married. and childless. From another source came
the information that, not unfrequently, a number of women
go together to a *menhir* accompanied by men armed with
sticks and stones who form a cordon round them. These
latter would (the narrator said) certainly attack and mal-
treat any man who dared to approach the spot. In some
districts these upright blocks of stone called *menhirs* have
been placed in rows of ten or more lines, thus forming an
avenue leading to a Dolmen or tomb of some ancient chief
and his family. Other stones, again, have been placed singly
in elevated positions, and are somewhat conical in form.
They much resemble the Śaiva stones of India.

The late Rev. W. C. Lukis, in his *Guide to the Chambered
Burrows of South Brittany*, when speaking of an enormous
menhir near Locmariaquer, now broken into three fragments,
but which would, if entire, be 67 feet 6 inches long, 13 feet
6 inches in its widest part, and 7 feet 6 inches thick, says :
"About 658 A.D. the Council of Nantes decreed that all
venerated stones or objects of superstitious devotion amongst
the people should be demolished. Some have thought that
this *menhir* was rudely thrown down and broken in pieces
in obedience to the order of this Council; others again,
that it either fell or was injured by lightning."

The following description of a cromlech on the island of
Anglesea by Captain Lukis, brother of the above-quoted
author, is a most interesting one in the present connection.
Captain Lukis, who is of opinion that such monolithic
monuments in Great Britain were connected with the

religious worship of the prehistoric stone builders, wrote in 1860 : " I have had another day at Brin-celle Dhu, as it is styled on the Ordnance map, or Yr Ogof (the cave) as it is called, on the island of Anglesea. I 'found a rude pavement of rough slabs, and immediately beneath it a thick bed of small beach pebbles." This is similar to the flooring of some of the dolmens in Brittany. Captain Lukis continues : " I also measured an extraordinary stone pillar which is on the right side of the chamber, in a slanting direction towards the south, and found it to be exactly nine feet in length, with a circumference in its thickest part—for it tapers upwards—of 14 feet 10 inches. This leaning pillar bore evidence of having been disturbed at the base on the southern side, but I do not conceive that when in its proper upright position it could have reached the under surface of the covering stones. On reasoning of the singularity of this pillar within the principal chamber, so very unlike the props of construction around the place, it cannot be considered to be for the purpose assigned to stone pillars or supports, which are sometimes found in cromlechs. In the monument of Dehus (or de Tus) in the island of Guernsey, the rude pillar beneath the second cap-stone was evidently placed there to support a flaw or crack which was found to endanger the covering stone ; — in other instances also, this has been the case — but in all of them the reason of the cromlech builders is clear and evident. At Yr Ogof we find a pillar with a regular abraded surface, *almost polished* in some parts, and gradually reduced upwards. Its character is so different from those on record that we are forced to assign some other reason for its introduction into the main chamber. Another abraded pillar stands at the eastern end of the avenue covered way. It is more rude and irregular than that of the chamber, and stands near a small side cist, which appears to be an addition to the chief cromlech. . . . I can only say that the pillars at Yr Ogof assimilate greatly with the *styles* of the Hindûs, although there may be some deeper meaning in placing them within the chamber of the dead."

Plate XI is a sketch of a *menhir* discovered some years ago near Pont l'Abbé in Brittany. It was found buried in a field near the village of Lescomil, and is now in the grounds of the Chateau de Kernuz, belonging to Mons. de Chatellain. The height of this monument is about 10 feet, it is about 4 feet 2 inches in diameter at the base, and 18 inches in diameter at the top. Its base is encircled by sculptured figures, each about 4 feet 3 inches in height, and arranged in four compartments. In one is a figure of Mercury, in another of Hercules, in a third of Mars, and in a fourth, which is much defaced, are the figures of Venus and Adonis (?). On Plate VIII, figs. 1 and 3, are representations of two rude sculptured stones in the island of Guernsey. Fig. 1, the Lady of St Martin's, as it is called, now stands at the entrance to St Martin's Churchyard, and fig. 3 is beneath a tree in the churchyard of Câtel parish. This latter was found a few years ago under the flooring of the Chancel of Câtel Church, when it was being relaid. It is similar in character to the Lady of St Martin's, but is much more defaced.

One cannot fail to be struck with the great resemblance in type which these two figures bear to those from Tartary and Greece, shown on Plate VII.   On Plate VIII, fig. 2, is a monolith from the Parish of St Peter's in the Wood, Guernsey.   Fig. 4 is a stone with a boss, upon which is an incised cross ; this is now let into a garden wall belonging to a house in St Martin's parish.   Fig. 5 is another incised stone built into an old archway at St Clare, on the same island.

Similar rude statues abound in the south of Russia.   On Plate IX, fig. 4, is a reproduction of a drawing sent to the writer from the neighbourhood of Ekaterinoslav.   Stone images of this character have also been found in great numbers on mounds in the Steppes.   Most of them are still upright, and as far as we have been able to learn, all are female figures.   The Russian lady who sent the drawing imagines 'they were not all intended to represent the same goddess—her reason being that these statues are all apparently of different dimensions and are not much alike, in so far as their obliterated features allow a likeness to be traced.   The hair behind, too, is not always arranged in the same manner : some have one plait, others two plaits, not unfrequently tied together at the ends.'

She also adds : " These idols were certainly worshipped in our country (Russia) at a very remote period, and it is even thought that human beings were sacrificed to them, because in many places quantities of bones have been found heaped up near them."   The statues are from seven to eight feet in height, but it has been impossible to ascertain of what kind of stone they are made.   The only information secured on this head is, that the material is of a dark brown colour, and has a yellowish tint in places ; also that the stone appears to be of a slightly porous nature. A singular fact was added—that neither this, nor any other kind of stone, exists on the Steppes in question. There is a great deal of granite in the bed of the Dneiper, but in the district now under discussion for hundreds of miles there is no material even for making roads ; yet an immense number of these statues on mounds are found there ; they are the only landmarks the traveller meets with.

Within the last few years the attention of Europeans in India has been drawn to the celts and other stone implements of various kinds and forms found there. Captain Lukis, who was in India at the time of the Mutiny, and had been accustomed from his earliest childhood to such objects, told us that during his residence there he recognised some near Allahâbâd, placed on a rectangular altar, built up of square stones and surmounted by a thin slab; from its centre rose a short *stylus*, against which five celts were leaning—three firmly fixed, and two detached.

Mr H. Rivett-Carnac, recently the head of the Opium Department in the North-West Provinces, and a keen observer of antiquarian objects during his annual camping tours over various parts of his district, has kindly permitted the use of a paper he wrote on this subject, published in the Journal of the Asiatic Society of Bengal for 1882. The celts figured on Plate XIII were all, we believe, found by him in the Banda district; their preservation is very possibly owing to their having been used as Śaiva stones. As far as this gentleman conducted his investigations, no such stone implements have been found in use at the present day, even amongst the most backward of the aboriginal tribes in India.

None of the natives of whom he made enquiries seemed to understand or to be able to explain their use ; they seemed rather to regard them as wonderful, mysterious, and even holy—in fact, with the same feeling that they look upon anything old and rare,—just as of certain beads which they occasionally find in Oudh after the rains.   The people say, " We did not make them, God made them."

Where turned up deep out of the earth by the plough, the celt is supposed by them to be a thunderbolt fallen from heaven.   The finder usually places it under the village pîpal tree (*ficus religiosa*), sometimes sanctifying it with a daub of red paint, and thus converting it into one of the emblems of Śiva.

Curious to relate, the older people in the island of Guernsey, when they find a celt, also look upon it as a thunderbolt.   It is said that the younger generation is becoming more enlightened, and that this superstition is by degrees dying out. On Plate XIV are figured celts found in Guernsey, for comparison with those of India.   A friend of the writer's (now deceased), when formerly residing on the island of Sark, was given a small celt by a farmer, which this man and his wife firmly believed was a thunderbolt.   It came to light in the following manner :—During a heavy thunderstorm, one of the farmer's cows, which was grazing in a field, was struck on the shoulder by the lightning, and killed instantaneously.   The animal was afterwards found sunk on its knees, stiff and rigid.   Its owner's immediate impulse was to dig into the earth round about the spot in order to find the thunderbolt which had caused the cow's death.   Strange to say, the celt, a very small green one, was found near the head of the animal; both the farmer and his wife thought that it had fallen from heaven, nor were the lady's reasonings of any avail in disabusing them of this idea.

On one of the carvings from the *Stûpa* at Sânchi, as reproduced by Fergusson in his *Tree and Serpent Worship*, is a figure holding an axe, which is fixed on to the handle by cross bands, in the same manner in which it is believed the stone celts were hafted. Mr Cockburn, Mr Rivett-Carnac's coadjutor in his labours, found a carving at Kâlañjar, which is evidently very ancient. It represents a human figure, holding in the right hand an implement which closely resembles a stone celt fixed into a wooden handle. One of the smaller celts found by Mr Rivett-Carnac he caused to be fixed into a handle of stag's horn, like those found in the Swiss lake dwellings. He had it sharpened, and said that it chopped wood as efficiently as a small iron axe.

In this paper Mr Rivett-Carnac seems at a loss to conceive how a very large celt in his collection, weighing more than eight pounds, could have been hafted and used as an instrument of that nature. This object, we would suggest, was most probably not intended for use, but for ornament, and was affixed to a bamboo or other pole, and placed in front of the hut of a chief as a symbol of authority. Equally large celts have been found in Scandinavia. The Director of the Ethnological Museum in Copenhagen conjectured that such was their use. This idea has subsequently received confirmation, from the fact that in a private collection in Guernsey are some colossal celts brought from the South Sea Islands by one who had seen them so employed.

On Plate XIII, fig 9, is represented a polished celt, which, from its form, is one of the most interesting in Mr Rivett-Carnac's collection.   It has two notches about half-way from the cutting edge, which were evidently made for the purpose of binding it to a handle, and the opposite directions of the planes of the notches indicate that the binding was carried round it.   In India, in Scandinavia, in Brittany, and in the Channel Islands, the stone of which the celts have been made is of various kinds, and consequently of various degrees of hardness.   Some are of sandstone, others of flint or of diorite, others again of hard black basalt, or of a kind of stone which does not exist at all in the neighbourhood in which they have been found—*e.g.*, a celt which was found in Guernsey is made of a material known to exist in no nearer country than Hungary, which would seem to indicate that certain implements of this nature were much prized, and carried about on the person.   The manufacture of celts gradually increased in perfection.   The earliest specimens had no polish, but to some of the later ones, in spite of the hardness of the material, a very high degree of finish has been given.   In Captain Lukis' collection is a most beautiful and typical celt of this kind ; it is made of a very hard kind of stone, deeply grooved on either side, and highly polished.   The Comte de Limur, a well-known French antiquarian, has said of some of the Indian celts, that they so closely resemble in this respect those dug out of the tumuli at Carnac and other parts of Brittany, that had they not been marked out for him, he would not have been able to distinguish the one from the other.

One or two partly polished celts have been found in the South Mirzâpur district in India.   They are about the length of the forefinger, and resemble in shape and size a jade knife from the Lake dwellings of Constance. This is now in the Indian Museum for comparison with the Indian types.

Sometimes a number of ordinary celts are found in India, heaped up near or beneath a pîpal tree ; these the owners are said to readily part with, but they will not give up any which they have decorated with colour.

It is well known that the Buddhists of Western Tibet and of the Lahaul valley make walls of stones at the entrances to their villages ; they are styled *Manis,* and are occasionally a quarter of a mile in length, but never more than four feet in height, and the same in width.

The natives of the Hangrang district in the Satlaj valley, and wherever Buddhism prevails in the Western Himâlayas (to which part only our knowledge extends), invariably pass these heaps of stone so as to have them on their right hand. Even when carrying heavy loads they will go some little distance out of their way up or down a mountain in order that they may pass them on their right hand. Numerous inscribed stones are loosely laid on the top of such walls ; they have been placed there as memorials of the dead, when starting on a journey, registering a vow, or entering upon any important undertaking. Should a person require one for any of the above-named purposes, he chooses a smooth stone and takes it to one of the local monasteries, where a Lama engraves upon it the sacred sentence, "*A UM maṇi padmê hûṁ,*" which has been translated to mean, " All hail to the jewel in the flower of the lotus." A UM or Ôṁ is a mystic syllable among the Hindûs signifying the supreme god of gods ; the Brahmans hesitate to pronounce this word aloud, and in doing so place one of their hands before their mouth so as to deaden the sound.

A sect called the Smârta Brahmans may be distinguished from other Brahmans by three horizontal marks of pounded sandal-wood on their foreheads and a round spot in the centre. They worship the triad of Brahma, Śiva, and Vishnu, under the mystical syllable AUṀ, and while admitting them to be co-equal, exalt Śiva as their chief deity.   They are also called *Advaitas* (*advait*, unique, alone), as they believe God and matter to be identical, and that everything is but an atom of the divinity—they themselves being parts of the Supreme Being.   The founder of this sect was Śankarâchârya, and their Guru or teacher, is styled the Śringiri-swâmi.

In this invocation A, the first letter, stands for the Creator; U, the second, for the Preserver; and M, the third, for the Destroyer—or Brahma, Vishnu, Śiva.   An old passage in the Purânas says : " All the rites ordained in the Vedas, the sacrifices to fire, and all sacred purifications shall pass away, but the word AUṀ shall never pass away, for it is the symbol of the Lord of all things."

We would claim that the formula, " *Ôṁ maṇi padmê hûṁ*," belongs both to the Hindû and the Buddhist : that both have adopted it and illustrated it in their own manner. From its peculiar mode of shedding its seeds, the natives of India have always regarded the lotus as the emblem of creative power.   From all time it has been held sacred by them, and might consequently be considered by Buddhists a suitable receptacle in which to deposit such a precious relic as a tooth of Buddha, which the Buddhists of Ceylon believe they possess.   It is kept in a temple at Kandy, within seven or more cases of gold or silver gilt, in the form of a *stûpa* or tumulus, each diminishing in size ; the tooth itself rests on a golden lotus flower ; it is most highly venerated, and but rarely exhibited to the public gaze. Europeans who have seen it, suppose from its size and its shape that it may be the tooth of an alligator.

That the Hindûs of the Śaiva sect have also adopted this formula seems apparent from a curious old brass object in the writer's collection, bought in the brass bazar at Benares. At the base is a bull, one of the emblems of Śiva ; from the back of the animal rises a lotus bud, which, on a couple of turns being given to it, expands, opens its petals, and discloses a small agate egg or bean. On the platform behind the bull is a cobra, with its body erect as if in the act of striking. It has a ring in its mouth which serves as a support to a small pointed vase perforated at its lower end. If this vessel be filled with water, the liquid drops slowly upon the egg in the centre of the flower, and thus a libation is poured on the *jewel in the flower of the lotus*.

About the word *Maṇi*, as signifying a sacred stone or line of stones : it seems to survive in Europe in place names. If we study a local map of Brittany, we cannot fail to be struck with the frequent recurrence of *mané* as the prefix to various sites on which are *dolmens* or megalithic monuments.

M. Henri Martin, in his *Études Archæologiques Celtiques*, explains *mané* to be the augmentation of the Celtic word *men* or *maen* stone—*e.g.*, *menhir*, great stone. He adds, that it designates equally an artificial mound or the summit of a mountain.

CHAPTER VII

SOME IDEAS ABOUT A FUTURE LIFE

WHEREVER the doctrine of annihilation has not prevailed, mankind has had in all ages, and still retains, the belief that the soul and the body are distinct, and that the soul has to go through a process of purification or a season of probation after the decease of the body, in order to atone for the evil deeds committed by the latter when on earth. This idea is most widely spread. We find it amongst Muhammedans and Hindûs, amongst the ancient Greeks, in Sweden, in Germany, in Northern America, on the island of Formosa, in the Fiji Islands, and in many other portions of the world. The process of atonement in a future world implies a journey thither; the nature of that journey has naturally been a source of speculation, and thence of belief, which in its turn has given rise to ceremonies mainly aimed at giving relief to the traveller along the dreadful and unknown road.

Ancestor worship in some form prevails amongst certain races in India—the people of the province of Coorg, for example.

Mr Conder, in his *Views of all Religions*, shows that this cult is not unknown amongst some so-called Christian peoples at the present day. He states, that "in the Armenian cemetery at Constantinople, which overlooks the Bosporus, whole families, consisting of two or three generations, may often be seen sitting round the tombs holding visionary communications with their deceased relatives and friends. According to their belief, the souls of the dead pass into a place called *Gayank*, which is not a purgatory, for they suffer neither pain nor pleasure, but retain a perfect consciousness of the past; and they believe also that they may be delivered from this state by the alms and prayers of the living, which are liberally contributed by pious Armenians. Easter Monday is their great day of assembly for this purpose, but every Sunday and some week days are frequently devoted to this purpose."

We will now consider that form of the ghostly journey in which the survivors deem it necessary that the body of the deceased should pass over water. Thus the Greeks had their Styx, Akherôn, and Kôkytus, over which souls were ferried by Kharon; it was their custom to plant asphodel around the tombs of the deceased, as its seeds were believed to be capable of affording nourishment to the dead.

A singular custom prevails in Greece at the present day. All corpses, whether of young or old, are carried through the streets in open coffins, attired as in life. The lid of the coffin is carried before it. This usage, it is said, was imposed upon them by the Turks when their land was under Turkish rule, with the object of preventing any living person being conveyed out of the country in a surreptitious manner. It would appear now to have become an established custom in that country.

The soul of the dead was supposed to journey to the under world by a *water progress*. This notion of a journey by water after death is common also to savage races at the present day. The inhabitants of the island of Formosa imagine that the souls of wicked men are tormented after death, and cast headlong into a bottomless pit of mire and dirt, and that the souls of the virtuous pass with pleasure and safety over it upon a narrow bamboo bridge which leads directly to a gay paradise where they revel in all kinds of sensual enjoyment; but that when the souls of the wicked attempt to pass this bridge they fall over on one side of it. Some of the American Indians have a tradition that they must go southwards to seek the land of Souls. According to the Eurocs, an untutored tribe in Northern California, the bright rivers, sunny slopes, and great forests of their paradise are separated from the earth by a deep chasm, which both good and wicked alike must cross on a thin slippery pole. The former soon reach the goal, guided doubtless by the Good Spirit as well as by the fire lighted on the grave by mourning friends, but the latter have to falter unaided along the shivering bridge, and many are the nights that pass before their friends venture to dispense with the beacon, lest the soul miss the path and fall into the dark abyss. Nor do they hold that retribution ends with the peril and anxiety of the passage, for they think that many are liable to return to the earth as birds, beasts, and insects. After forty years' residence as a Missionary in Samoa, one of the Pacific islands, Dr George Turner, in a work published a few years since, says, " That the inhabitants of that island held that the souls of dead Samoans started for Pulstu, the spirit world, through two circular holes near the beach, the larger hole being for the souls of chiefs, and the lesser one for those of commoners. They went under the sea till they came to a land where all things were very much as they had been on earth; chiefs looked forward with pride to the use of their bodies as pillars in the house of the Samoan Pluto."

It is still a very common notion in the East that the souls of the dead must pass over water or over a bridge before they can arrive at their final resting-place. In the native state of Chamba, in the Panjab Himâlayas, there is such a bridge over which all corpses must be carried on their way to the burning ghât near the river where the bodies are cremated, and though there is another perfectly easy and straight path, the bearers of the dead always traverse this perilous causeway, which is in the form of a high arch of considerable length, and hardly more than eighteen inches wide. It is not protected at the sides in any way. The people of Chamba are Hindûs.[1]

The Muhammedans have also their Sirât, a sharp bridge, which they believe to be laid over the middle of hell, and which must be crossed by all at the close of the solemn judgment, whether they are destined for Paradise or for the place of torment. The same notion is also found in the Zoroastrian and the Jewish systems, whence no doubt Muhammed borrowed it. Their profession of faith in this runs as follows: "We most heartily believe and hold for certain that all mankind must go over the sharp bridge which is as long as the earth, and no broader

---

[1] This custom most probably arose from the old Hindû belief in Vaitarani, the swift river of hell, composed of filth, blood, and ordure, which must be crossed by holding on to a cow's tail as it swims over, a belief which has given rise to many death customs in use at the present day.

than the thread of a spider's web, and of a height propor-
tionate to its length.   The just shall pass it like lightning,
but the wicked, for want of good works, will be an age in
performing it.   They will fall and precipitate themselves
into hell fire with blasphemers and infidels, with men of
little faith and bad conscience, with those who have not
had virtue enough to give alms.   Yet some just persons
will get over it quicker than others, who will now and then
be tried upon the commands which they have not duly
observed in this life.   How dreadful will this bridge appear
to us! what virtue, what inward grace of the Most High
will be required to get over it!   How earnestly shall we
not look for this favour!   What deserts, what venomous
creatures shall we not find on our road!   What hunger,
drought, and weariness shall we endure!   What anxiety,
grief, and pain shall attend those who do not think of this
dangerous passage!   Let us beg of God to grant us with
bodily health the grace not to go out of this life loaded
with debts, for the Arabians often say, and with good
reason, that no obstacle is so hidden as that which we
cannot overcome by any expedient or artificial contrivance
whatever."

Connected with death ceremonies in Asia is an attendant
dog.   The Pârsîs place a dog in the chamber of a dying
person to serve as the soul's escort to heaven.   According
to their belief, the soul arrives at the bridge of Chinvat,
where the gods and the unclean spirits fight for the possession of it.   If the soul be that of a righteous person it is
defended by the other pure souls and by the dogs that
guard the bridge.

Some Ideas about a Future Life 105

In Buddhist countries, too, a somewhat similar idea prevails. A very large and savage breed of dogs is kept in certain of the *Lamasaraïs* or Monasteries in order that they may eat the bodies of the dead. This is deemed the most honourable form of burial in Ladakh or Western Tibet, and is of course reserved for the rich. The corpses of the poorer class are either placed in the river or deposited on the tops of the mountains to be devoured by wild animals or birds of prey.

In 1876, when passing through Lama Yuru, a few marches from Léh, we went over the Lama monastery there. Some of these fierce dogs tried to spring out upon our party. It seemed to us that even their owners could not trust them, and had much difficulty in restraining their ferocious instincts.

A very curious instance of the idea that some form of absolution is necessary after death for sins done in the body occurred in India in the fourteenth century; the actors were Muhammedans. Tughlaqâbâd, near the modern city of Delhi, was founded by Ghiyasû'd-din Tughlaq Shâh, who reigned 1321-1325 A.D., and was succeeded by his son, Muhammad Shâh Tughlaq, an accomplished prince, but a man most unscrupulous in his actions. He is credited with having, among other crimes, compassed the death of his father. When he came to the throne, he was the most inhuman and tyrannical of all the Pathân sovereigns of India, and many of his cruelties were witnessed by his cousin, Firoz Shâh Tughlaq—also called Bârbak—who ascended the throne on his death in 1351 A.D., and sought by a singular method to cancel some of his predecessor's sins. The words of Firoz himself, as related by Ferishtah, who took them from an inscription on a large mosque at Firozâbâd, are as follows: "I have taken pains to discover the surviving relations of all persons who suffered from the wrath of my late Lord and Master, Muhammad Tughlaq, and having pensioned and provided for them, have caused them to grant their full pardon and forgiveness to that prince, in the presence of the holy and learned men of this age, whose signatures and seals as witnesses are affixed to the documents; the whole of which, as far as lay in my power, have been procured and put into a box and deposited in the vault in which Muhammad Tughlaq is entombed." These papers were intended to serve as vouchers of free pardon from all whom the dead man had caused to be deprived of a nose, of a limb, or of sight, and were placed near him in order that he might pick them up at the last day, for according to Muhammedan belief, every offence has a double aspect, in its relation first to God and then to man. In the latter case, pardon given by the injured one is believed to reduce some portion of its future punishment.

It has been stated that a somewhat similar custom is in use amongst the Christians of the Greek Church, and that they are in the habit of putting into the hands of a deceased person at his interment a written form of absolution, which is understood to be a discharge in full from all the sins which he has committed during life.[1]

The notion of certifying to the Deity the virtues of the

[1] Closely allied to this is the poetical idea prevalent in the Tyrol, that if two people say the same thing at the same time they have redeemed a soul.

deceased is a widely spread one. It is said to be customary amongst the Laplanders for six of the most intimate friends of the deceased to place the body in a coffin, after wrapping it in linen with the face and hands left uncovered. In one hand they put a purse with some money to pay the fee of the porter at the gates of Paradise, in the other a certificate signed by the priest, directed to St Peter, to witness that the dead person was a good Christian. A superstition of the same nature is held by the people of the Fiji Islands. They worship a god they call Ndengei under the form of a large serpent, and believe that immediately after death the spirit of the deceased person goes to him for purification or to receive sentence, but that it is not permitted, however, to all spirits to reach the judgment seat of Ndengei. They say that an enormous giant armed with an axe is constantly upon the watch on the road thither, ready to attack and wound all that attempt to reach him, and that no wounded person can go forward to Ndengei, but is doomed to wander about in the mountains. To escape unscathed from the giant's axe is ascribed solely to good luck. Another development of this idea is to be found in India, where a portion of the *pújá* or worship gone through occasionally by Hindûs is called *tarpan*. It is a form of absolution for the souls of deceased ancestors and friends : it can be performed by the male sex only. The Brâhmans have long ago made use of the notion of the necessity for providing for the needs of a future life to further their own present comforts, and Maurice rightly remarks : " Great rewards are promised to those that are charitable (towards the Brâhmans), inasmuch as they believe that if a man performs the first kind of *dân* (*pûjâ* or worship, which consists in giving away his own weight in gold or silver), he is ordained to remain in Paradise for one hundred million *kalpas* or periods of Brahmâ, and that when he reassumes a human form he will become a mighty monarch." This particular phase of "good works" has in modern times taken a most eccentric and objectionable form. There is a class of Hindû ascetics in the Pañjâb who called themselves Suthrashâhis, from their founder, a Brahman named Sucha, who lived in the time of Aurangzeb (1658 to 1707 A.D.). Their legend is, that hearing that he could perform wonders, the Emperor summoned the faqir to his presence, and told him that any favour he might ask should be granted, on which he requested that he and his followers might be permitted to go about begging unmolested and freely, and that every shopkeeper should be made to pay them not less than one *paisa* (about a halfpenny). His followers still continue their profitable trade, and are noted for their indolence, intemperance, and excesses. They carry two short sticks and walk through the bazars beating these together until money is given them ; nor will they pass on till they get it, sitting *dharnâ*, as it is called, for hours or even days till their demands are satisfied. On receiving alms, they say to the shopkeeper, " May Bâbâ Nânak Shâh (the founder of the Sikh religion) take your boat safely over the river of life."

The Burmese, it is said, hold that a funeral should never go to the north or the east. Their graveyards are usually situated to the west of their villages ; it is their custom that the dead should be carried out of a walled town by a gate set apart for that purpose. In Mandelay this gate is to the south-west ; it is avoided as cursed.

The Egyptians also placed their land of the dead to the west. Whenever it was possible their tombs were on the west bank of the Nile. The Nile was crossed, and when they were on the eastern shore the procession passed over a sacred lake. As the mourners passed on, the constant cry was, " To the West, to the West." The soul of the dead man was supposed to journey to the under world by a water progress.

The necessity for an attendant dog is a superstition held in the west as well as in the east. It is a popular belief throughout all that part of France which formed the ancient Armorica, that the dead betake themselves at the moment of their departure to the parish priest of Braspar, whose dog escorts them to Great Britain. To this day it is said to be the custom in the parish of Plougnel, on the river Treguire in Brittany, for corpses to be conveyed to the churchyard by boat over a narrow arm of the sea called *Passage de l'Enfer*, instead of taking them by the shorter land route. In Scandinavian mythology, a fabulous dog called Garmr was believed to guard the entrance to the infernal regions. Several of the northern nations of Europe believed the dead had to cross over water in boats to their future home.

For this reason, in Scandinavia, bodies were sometimes buried in ships. A large vessel containing the bones and weapons of some deceased chief was found a few years ago near the Sonde Fjord in Norway. Sweden, too, has popular legends to the same effect. Thus, Odin is fabled to have conveyed the slain from Brahalla to Valhalla in a golden ship. In Germany, again, popular opinion of old assigned Great Britain, as being across the water, to be the Land of Souls.

CHAPTER VIII

SACRED TREES

In the book of Revelation (Chap. XXII) is mentioned "the tree of life, which bore twelve manner of fruits and yielded her fruit every month, and the leaves of the tree were for the healing of the nations." One of the notions of the primitive Aryan cosmogony was that of a prodigious tree which overshadowed the whole world.

On a fragment of a terra-cotta vase in the Museum of Antiquities at Copenhagen—it is supposed to belong to the later Bronze Age—is figured a tree which the late Kāmer Herr Dr Worsaae called the tree of life. It is present in connection with Sun symbols. A similar tree symbol has been found in Ireland at New Grange, Drogheda.

It is most interesting to find the symbol of the tree with its twelve leaves, or occasionally the same number of flowers or fruits, on Persian carpets to this day. To quote Sir George Birdwood's *Industrial Arts of India*, in which he says, " In Yarkand carpets the tree is seen filling the whole centre of the carpet stark and stiff as if cut out in metal. In Persian art, and in Indian art derived from the Persian, it becomes a beautiful flowering plant, or a simple sprig of flowers ; in purely Hindû art it remains in its pure architectural form as seen in temple lamps and in the models in brass or copper of the sacred fig, as the tree of life." Two kinds of fig trees—the *Banian* (*ficus Indica*) and the *pîpal* (*ficus religiosa*) are held in India to be especially holy. The *pîpal* indeed is accounted so sacred that oaths are taken under its shade, and merchants will sometimes object to have one near their stalls or shops : they say that in such a case they could not ask more than a proper price for their goods. The Buddhists hold that it was beneath a tree of this species that Buddha attained *Nirvâna*[1]; and a descendant of the sacred tree (quite a young one), under which he is believed to have attained Buddahood, is still worshipped at Buddh-Gayâ. According to Buddhist tradition, it was once desired to send a branch of the original tree to Ceylon, but no knife could be permitted to touch it. In this dilemma the tree itself came to the rescue—a branch dropped off into the golden vessel which had been prepared for it.

Pietro della Valle, a Sicilian, who visited India in 1623, speaks of a tree outside the town of Cambay, of the same kind as those on the coast of Persia, near Hormazd, where it was called *lâl*. He adds that it is unknown in Europe, and that the Hindûs style it *bar* (*i.e.*, banian). This tree was held in great veneration. He goes on to say : " On account of its great size and antiquity, the people visit it frequently and honour it with the superstitious ceremonies belonging to their religion. It is dedicated to Pârbatî, the wife of Mahâdeo, or Śiva. At the trunk of this tree, not far from the ground, is a rudely sculptured circle, which does not in the least resemble the human countenance, but according to their ideas is the

---

[1] A state of complete holiness and rest according to some authorities : of annihilation or absorption into the Deity according to others.

face of their idol. They paint this circle a bright red colour. The Romans did the same, for Pliny relates that they covered the face of Jove with vermilion. Moreover, this sacred tree has always round it a circle of certain heart-shaped leaves; those belong to a plant which is here called *pân*, but in other parts of India *betel*."

Another instance of a peculiarly sacred fig tree is to be found in the fort at Allahâbâd, where there is a Hindû temple, which, owing to an accumulation of the soil, is some twenty feet below the present level of the ground, and can only be approached by descending a flight of steps. This temple is a great resort for pilgrims. Within it the priests show the stump of a tree of the fig species, which they say miraculously throws out leaves at a certain season of the year. When we saw it the stump was perfectly bare of leaves; it had three or four branches, each about four inches in diameter, and about three feet in length; these were clean cut at their upper extremities; neither the wood nor the bark looked like that of a dead tree. Every year, at the time of the large annual fair, which takes place at Allahâbâd, this tree, it is said, certainly has leaves; the seeming miracle is accounted for by the generally accepted belief (by Europeans) that the sergeant of the guard—it is a British fort—receives a bribe from the Brâhmans to open the gates the night previous to the commencement of the fair, in order to permit them to introduce a new tree.

A similar idea also existed formerly in Scandinavia. Tradition relates that near old Upsala, in Sweden, there was a sacred tree, which was always green; the same thing is also said of another tree on the island of Gothland.

In Scandinavia the trees most reverenced were the birch (which from its heart-shaped leaves, its pendulous branches, and its yellowish white bark, more nearly resembles the *pîpal* than any other European tree), the beech, the common ash, and the rowan or mountain ash. M. Holmböe, when speaking of tree worship in Scandinavia, says : " In Norway one still meets with trees which are reputed sacred. A magnificent birch tree on a farm in the parish of Sognedal, in the diocese of Bergen, deserves mention. The inhabitants of that place relate that no sharp instrument has ever touched that tree, and that anciently it was the custom, once a year, at Christmas to water it with fresh beer." We have here a combination of Buddhistic ideas and the Hindû custom of offering libations.

In the Himâlayas, where the *pîpal* does not flourish, the *deodâr*, a variety of the cedar, is the sacred tree, as its name, "the tree of the gods," implies. Groves of this tree have been planted near the principal temples both in the Satlaj and the Kulu valleys. The oak was the sacred tree of Great Britain ; its name in Gaelic is *darach*. It was also sacred to Thor, the Scandinavian god of Fire, because of the red colour of its fresh-cut bark. In Mexico and in Central America cypresses and palms used to be grown near the temples, generally in groups of three. They were tended with great care, and often received offerings of incense and other gifts ; but they do not seem to have been dedicated to any particular god, as amongst the Romans, where Pluto was given the cypress and Victory the palm.

Mention has been made by some writers on America of a cypress at Santa Maria di Tule, which was one of the most sacred of South American trees; its trunk is said to have measured ninety feet in circumference at a height of six feet from the ground. In Europe "sacred trees" have been put to a more practical use; instances innumerable could be given in which in ancient times European courts of justice and other public assemblies were illegal, unless held in the open air beneath the shade of some tree, most frequently the oak. The same idea prevails in Africa among the people of the Congo, where the village chief and the members of his family form the legislative council, which meets under a tree: it is stated that the *ficus religiosa* is the tree selected for this purpose.

Many of the English Gospel oaks were planted to mark the parish boundaries, and it was beneath their shade that the clergyman read the Gospel on Ascension Day or Holy Thursday, when, with the parish officials and others, he assisted at the beating of the bounds. In fact, nearly all the celebrated oak trees in England were boundary trees—*e.g.*, the Shire Oak in Sherwood Forest, Notts. The beating of the bounds is still practised in some of the Metropolitan parishes. The procession consists of boys belonging to various charity and parish schools, dressed in quaint uniforms of a bygone time, and provided with long willow wands. They are headed by the parish clerk, beadle, and other functionaries. In some cases the procession passes through houses and workshops, and on the different spots being pointed out to them which divide their respective parishes, the lads strike the ground vigorously with their canes. They are afterwards generally regaled with buns and milk, granted a half-holiday, and given a small coin.

All the world over propitiatory and thank-offerings have been made to objects of worship. In Chapter VI. we have shown that with the Buddhists of Western Tibet, they are for the most part of the former character. Similarly the Hindûs at Ahmadâbâd in Gujarât hang up tiny horses made of white calico and stuffed with bran—these, however, more nearly resemble giraffes than horses—on the railings surrounding the tomb of a former Muhammedan ruler of that province before commencing any important work, imagining that they thus ensure its success.

Tavernier, who visited India in the time of the Emperor Akbar, mentions that in his time it was the custom for pilgrims going to a temple for the cure of any disease to bring with them figures or models of the parts affected, made either of gold, silver, or copper, according to their rank or ability, as offerings to the god. At Fathepur Sikri, near Agra, propitiatory offerings are made at the shrine of Salîm Chishtî, the friend of the Emperor Akbar. There certain Hindûs are in the habit of jumping off a high wall into a tank below, a distance of more than sixty feet, in order to amuse European visitors. A similar custom also obtains close to the tomb of Nizam'ud-dîn Auliya near Delhi. The men are said always to give a third or fourth part of whatever they receive for performing this feat to the shrine of the saint, whose tomb is in the courtyard. They are said to believe that were they to omit their offerings they would perish on their next attempt to make the leap.

Offerings to shrines soon extended to the trees in their neighbourhood : these were mostly of the nature of thank-offerings. Such votive offerings as an expression of thankfulness for blessings received may be seen in every Roman Catholic country : at *Lourdes* in the Pyrenees they number hundreds of thousands of various kinds. In many countries they may be seen at shrines by the wayside and as pictures hung up on trees.

At Nâgkanda (or the shoulder of the snake), a place in India about forty miles north of Simla, there are several small trees and shrubs on the highest part of a low mountain pass decorated with numerous votive rags. These streamers are of various colours : they are, it is said, thank-offerings placed there by native travellers on attaining the summit of the hill—a rather perilous journey in the winter for those coming from the north.

In his *Travels in the East, more particularly Persia* (published in 1821), Sir William Ouseley writes : " Barbaro, who went to Persia, as the Venetian envoy, two centuries earlier than either Chardin or Angelo, observed in his journey through Persia some thorn bushes to which were attached vast numbers of old rags and scraps of garments. These were (as was supposed) efficacious in banishing fevers and other disorders. The Persians, who are Muhammedans, and abhor idolatry in any form, still continue to imagine that, in their addresses and offerings to these trees, they only invoke the true God."

In another place the same author speaks of a monolith, about ten feet high, at a place called Tang-i-Karm in Persia, surrounded by a dwarf wall to denote its sacredness. The top of this stone was hollowed out, as he thought, for fire ; it was locally known as the stone of the fire temple. On a tree near it he found remnants of garments left there as votive

offerings by superstitious persons. Again, in Vol. II. Chap.
VIII, when describing the journey he made from Shiraz to
Fapa and Darab, he speaks of having met with a stone altar
surrounded by a rude stone wall or fence of large stones. He
says of this place : " Near it there were a few trees, none of
them remarkable for their size, but most of them apparently
old. Amongst them was a *Dirakht-i-fazl*, the branches of
which were thickly hung with rags, as high as a man's arm
could reach." He continues : " This name *dirakht-i-fazl* (the
excellent tree) is bestowed on every tree that exhibits votive
offerings, without regard to its size, species, age, beauty, or
situation. Such trees are found near the tombs of supposed
saints (or *Imâm-Zadehs*), though they may frequently be seen
in desert places, where they could not be supposed to have
derived sanctity from such relics."

The poet and philosopher Sa'adi (born in the twelfth
century), in his work entitled *Gulistân, or the Rose Garden*,
speaks of a sacred tree to which the people commonly
resorted to offer up petitions.

From some of their sacred books, which the Gabrs and
Pârsîs attribute to Zaratusht (Zoroaster) himself, but which
are supposed to have been compiled in the third century A.D.,
from ancient MSS. and traditions, it appears that trees were
invoked by them as *pure* and *holy*, and that a form of prayer
was particularly addressed to the Feroüers (Fravashis)—
spirits of saints—through whose influence the trees grew up
in purity, and who, placed above those trees as on a throne,
were occupied in blessing them. Some of these Feroüers
are described as females ; all are immortal and powerful, but
beneficent and pleased with offerings. They protect their

votaries, and are prompt in carrying up to the mighty Ormuzd the petitions of those who invoke them.

Holed stones and trees form a curious subject for speculation. The key to the secret seems to have been hit upon by Maurice in his *Indian Antiquities*, where he says : " The Indians are in the habit of purifying themselves by passing through a natural or artificial cavern, where the spiritual pilgrims enter at the south gate, and make their exit at the northern one, as was anciently the custom in the Mithraic mysteries." In India, in pursuance of this notion, certain stones which have natural holes in them are regarded as sacred. Those persons, or children who pass through such holes, are held to receive thereby a " New birth of the Soul." Under the same idea, the rulers of Travancore, in Southern India, who are Nâyars by caste, are made into Brâhmans when they ascend the throne by passing through a golden cow or lotus flower, which then becomes the property of the Brâhman priests. The idea of a spiritual or bodily new birth probably controls the modern customs as regarding certain pillars in the courtyard of the Mosque of 'Umar at Cairo, two of which are much closer together than any of the rest. The natives say of these that only an honest or a good man (one new born ?) can pass between them.

We now turn to Europe. We shall see that there, in some countries, and also with us in Great Britain, the belief in holed stones, in natural or purposely split trees, is not yet extinct.

On our continent the purposely distorted branch of a tree, as well as the naturally or artificially perforated stone, seems to have been used for the purpose of curing diseases,

and thereby producing, as it were, a " New birth of the
Body." In 1883, when staying with some Danish friends at
their country house, situated some ten or twelve miles from
Roeskilde, one day during our drive we passed through some
extensive woods. At one point an old beech tree was shown
us, one branch of which, at a height of about a foot from the
ground, formed a perfect bow ; higher up again it was united
to the main trunk of the tree. It had most probably been
operated upon when quite young, by a portion of the trunk
being split and held open by wedges. Our hosts informed
us that, to their certain knowledge, up to within eight years
previously parents who had sick children were in the habit of
coming there from considerable distances in order to pass
their little ones through this hole, believing that thereby their
maladies would be cured. The ceremony was not complete,
however, till they had torn a strip of cloth from the child's
dress and tied it to this branch of the tree, in the belief that
when this decayed or was borne away by the wind the little
sufferer would be healed : showing thereby one use of the
rag bush. Our friends added, that occasionally many such
streamers might be seen hanging on this tree at one time.

Gilbert White of Selborne says that, in his time, there
stood at that place " A row of pollard ashes which by the
long seams and cicatrices down their sides, manifestly show
that in former times they had been cleft asunder. These trees,
when young, were severed and held open by wedges, whilst
sick children stripped naked were passed through the aper-
tures, under the persuasion that by such a process the poor
babies would be cured. As soon as the operation was over,
the tree in the suffering part was plastered over with loam

and carefully swathed up. If the part coalesced and soldered together, as usually fell out when the feat was performed with any adroitness at all, the infant was cured, but where it still continued to gape, it was supposed that the method used would prove ineffectual." "We have," he goes on to say, "several persons now living in the village, who, in their childhood, were believed to have been healed by this super- stitious ceremony, derived, perhaps, from our Saxon ancestors, who practised it before their conversion to Christianity." It is said that a similar custom is still in vogue as regards the ash tree in some of the southern counties of England, and that there also children suffering from whooping-cough are made to pass through the loop, formed by a bramble which has taken root at both ends.

In his *Folk-Lore of the Northern Counties of England*, Mr Henderson cites a custom in use at St Helen's Well, near Thorp Arch, in Yorkshire, where "the offering was a scrap of cloth fastened to an adjoining thorn, which presented a strange appearance under its bundle of rags."

In Ireland, also, trees situated near holy wells are adorned in the same manner. Close to the churchyard of Durrow, a village about three miles and a half from Tulla- more, is a grove of horse chestnut trees, and beneath these a holy well. On a branch near the well there are numerous rags hung up by superstitious people, in the belief that a rag moistened with this blessed water, wound round a sore, and when removed hung on the tree, will take away the sore. At the *Pattern* (or feast) at this village, the priest, we were told, explains to the people all about the holy well and the blessed tree. The well is covered over with a stone arch,

on which rests a thin slab, inserted over the well door. It
bears the following inscription : " Saint Columba used this
well when he preached the Gospel and built an Abbey here,
A.D. 550. Here angels shall enjoy my sacred cell, my Sloe,
my Nut, mine Apple among wells." The graveyard is about
eighty or ninety years old, the well cover about forty or fifty
years.

Two important examples of holed stones are described by
the late Rev. W. C. Lukis in his *Prehistoric Monuments of the
British Isles*, published for the Society of Antiquaries, London,
1885. One of these, called the Tolven, situated near St Buryan,
has been used superstitiously within living memory for curing
infirm children of their diseases by passing them through it ;
the other, near Madron, is called the Men-an-Tol. Both are
on Plate XII. The Tolven, a slab of large dimensions, has a
hole sixteen and a half inches in diameter bored through its
centre ; this was made by picking away the opposite sides
equally. This stone was shifted from its original site by the
tenant of the house behind which it stands, in order to make
room for a pathway to his back door. The Men-an-Tol is
on the moors, a short distance to the right of Lanyon Farm-
house, in the direction of Kara Galva. The hole in this
latter stone is not a perfect circle, being twenty-one inches in
diameter in one direction and eighteen inches in the other.
It stands exactly midway between two high stones, which are
in the same line with it in the direction N.-E. and S.-W.
The hole has been made in the same manner as that in the
Tolven—with this difference, the counter-sinking is not equal.
This, it is obvious, was intentional—the deeper sinking
is on the eastern side of the stone. One of the most in-

teresting features of these monuments is the names by which they are known; *men* or *maen* is the word for stone both in Brittany and in Wales to this day, and in the word Tolven we find both the Welsh and the Norwegian word for a hole. There is a mountain in Norway called Tolhattan, which has an enormous natural hole in it about 200 to 300 feet above sea level. When viewed from a ship, as we saw it, the sky is seen through a vast square opening far above the spectator. A Norwegian friend told us that he had once walked through this hole—it took him a quarter of an hour; this gives some idea of its length, though it possibly might have been necessary for him to clamber rather than walk, for our informant added that the hole is gradually increasing in size owing to the rocks and stones which are constantly falling from its upper part.

Many curious superstitions exist on the island of Tiree in Scotland, the property of the Dukes of Argyll. On the west side is a rock with a hole in it, through which children are passed when suffering from whooping-cough and other complaints. Ripon Minster has beneath its central tower a crypt which goes by the name of St Wilfrid's Needle; it is entered from the nave by a narrow passage forty-five feet in length, and consists of a vaulted cell nine feet six inches high, seven feet nine inches wide, and eleven feet long. An opening in the north side of the cell, thirteen inches by eighteen, is called "The Needle." The original use for which this crypt and the singular opening were intended cannot now be ascertained with certainty, but there is a popular tradition that in former times the Needle was used as a "test." "They pricked their credits who could not thread the Needle," is the quaint remark of old Fuller in reference to the supposed use of the opening.

We can trace the origin of our Maypole and Maypole dances in parts of Southern India. When passing through native villages in the Dekhan, it is not uncommon to see several children dancing in a circle round an extemporised and decorated pole fixed in the ground. In the native theatre at Belgaum we saw the same dance got up most beautifully by a professional troupe. Though our Mayday dances seem to be almost a relic of the past, the custom of erecting a pole on the eve of Mayday still survives in some places in England, as we will proceed to show. A singular usage remains in several villages in the neighbourhood of Hereford. This custom would seem to have an original connection with Indian tree-worship. *Firstly*, from the nature of the pole used, a birch tree, which (probably for the reasons stated above) was the sacred tree of Scandinavia. *Secondly*, from the red colour of the rags and handkerchiefs (red is the Hindû sacred colour) attached to it as offerings. The cross-piece, judging from the virtues attributed to the whole, was very possibly a later addition. This latter, however, must consist of a branch of a kind of elder—a tree which in the British Isles and in other parts of Europe is accounted to possess special properties.

On the eve of Mayday, the farm labourers of several villages in that country are in the habit of erecting a high pole in their master's farmyard. They are said to hold that at that time witches and such folk are especially evil-disposed towards his live stock. This pole is invariably a young birch tree. Not far from the top, and thus forming a cross, is placed a branch of what the country people there-abouts call the *Wittern* tree (*Sambucus aquatica*), a species of elder. The birch pole is decorated with streamers of red-coloured rags or handkerchiefs. There would appear to be no rule as to how long the pole should remain up, but it must be in position on Mayday.

Holy trees, too, are not unknown in that country. On a farm in Blakemere Parish (about ten miles from Hereford) is a thorn tree which is said to blossom on Christmas eve at midnight. Our informant said he had been assured of this as a fact, but he had never himself seen it. In the parish of Kingstone, about seven miles from Hereford, in another direction, it was the custom a very few years ago to nail up two bits of wood—oak, we believe—in the form ✝ of the Greek cross over each of the house doors of the row of almshouses in that parish. When asked about this, the people said they did it with the object of scaring away witches or evil spirits. These crosses dis-appeared quite recently when the houses were repaired and whitewashed. Similar crosses are still to be seen over some of the house and stable doors in Kingstone.

In Worcester there is a superstition that it is a most unfortunate circumstance if a sick person's bed *crosses* the boards of their room. Its position should be changed at once ; they declare that otherwise the invalid is certain to die. " The church bells ring heavy," as they express it when a death is about to take place in the village. Another superstition belonging to that country is, that if a sprig of broom be brought into a house there will be a death in it before the year is out.

The Austrian Tyrol has its superstitions about trees. Everyone reverences the elder bush. The people say that the hat should be taken off to it as well as to the lime and the ash tree. At Verdins, near Meran, after felling a tree, the peasant carves three crosses upon the stump, in order that neither devil nor witches may sit upon it.

There is a legend in the Etsch Thal (Adige Valley) that once upon a time a plague raged there, and that thousands of people perished, until a peasant chanced to hear a bird which was perched on an elder bush sing the following words :—

> " Hattest du gess'n *Kranebilt* and *Bibernell*,
> Wärst du g'storb'n nit so g'schnell."

> " Had'st thou eaten *juniper* berries and *Pimpernella peregrina*,
> Thou wouldst not have died so quickly."

The peasant, it is said, took the hint, ate juniper berries, and after that no one died of the plague.

CHAPTER IX

SNAKE WORSHIP

SNAKE worship is still to be found in India throughout the length and breadth of the land, from Nâga-kovil (Temple of the Snake in the extreme south) to the frontiers of Central Asia; in fact, almost wherever there is a Hindû population, either its actual presence or its former existence may be seen or traced. Commencing at the extreme north, we find that the earliest form of religion in Kashmir is supposed to have been Nâga or snake worship, since when Buddhism, Hindûism, and again Nâga worship are said to have prevailed in that valley. At the time of its conquest by Akbar, in 1558 A.D., Abu'l-fazl relates that there were no less than seven hundred different places there where images of snakes were worshipped by the inhabitants, against one hundred and thirty-four dedicated to Śiva, sixty-four to Vishnu, twenty-two to Durgâ, and three to Brahmâ—a statement which is borne out by the character of the architecture of the valley, as we now see it; for with very few exceptions all the most ancient temples have been devoted to serpent worship.[1]

It seems highly probable that the *parâk* or head dress

[1] Some of them stand in courts capable of being flooded; they were entered by stone causeways; the drains have become choked up; they cannot now be approached except by wading. The temple at Pandrethan, near Srînagar, is a case in point. Mr Fergusson was of opinion that the temple at Martand also belonged to the sect of the Nâgas or snake worshippers; others, however, have thought that it was dedicated to the Sun.

worn by the women of Ladâkh (who are Buddhists) should be
held to be a remnant of serpent worship in the Himâlayas.
This ornament has precisely the form of a cobra ; the extremity
of the tail is fastened to the hair on the forehead, and the
broad flat hood of the snake descends behind to the waist of
the wearer. It is most usually made of leather, on which are
sewn at intervals rough pierced turquoises and brooches of
silver or gold, according to the wealth and position of the
wearer ; but every woman, however poor, possesses a *parâk*
of some kind.

Passing on southwards, we find that a special feast is
held one day only in the year at Benares, near the Bakarîyâ
Kund, in a suburb of that city, in honour of the serpent god.
Some of the forms under which the serpent is sculptured near
that spot are given on Plate XVI, figs. 1, 2, 3, 4, 5. Fig. 6 is
placed beside them for the sake of comparison ; the type is
the same ; this latter we found engraved on a stone in the
interior of a dolmen within a tumulus on Gavr Innis, an island
off the south coast of Brittany.

It should be observed that the name for the cobra in India
is Nâg or Nât. Certain spots in the province of Coorg in the
Southern Peninsula are called *Nâtas*. The natives believe that
cobras have died at these. According to them this creature lives
a thousand years ; at the expiration of five hundred years of
existence it begins to shrink, and becomes of a silvery brightness, diminishing always, so that when it attains the age of six
hundred or seven hundred years it is only one yard in length.
Later on still it becomes of a golden colour, and is then only
one foot long, and when it is reduced to only a few inches,
one fine day it rises up into the air, dies, and falls to the

ground and disappears. They believe that should any one by chance tread upon this spot he would be stricken with a grievous skin disease and die a horrible death.

There is a class of men in Coorg, a mongrel race called Kaniyas, who set themselves up as wizards and magicians. They make their rounds about the country, going sometimes to a landed proprietor and informing him that a cobra has died somewhere on his property. This latter is naturally anxious to avoid any evil consequences which might result, and for a consideration induces the Kaniya to indicate to him the exact spot, which he then carefully encloses with a low wall of stones.

It is remarkably singular to find in a Teutonic language the Indian word for a snake. It would seem scarcely necessary to remind our readers that the German word for a viper is *Natter*. At the foot of the Simplon, where the people are of German origin, is a little village called Naters, to which is attached the following legend :—Close to this village, on the mountain side, is a deep cavern, which tradition states was formerly inhabited by a horrible dragon (dragons and serpents are synonymous in such tales), who subsisted upon human flesh and any cattle or sheep which he could plunder. He daily devoured a shepherd or one of his flock. The tale goes on to relate that a blacksmith, who for some crime had been condemned to death, told the magistrate of the place, on the eve of his execution, that he would kill the dragon if he were promised a free pardon should he escape with his life from the encounter. The combat took place, the blacksmith using a sword which he had forged for the occasion. The battle lasted an hour or more, when the spectators, seeing that both man and dragon were prostrate on the ground, approached them, but with fear and trembling. They found both incapable of further effort—the dragon was dead and the man had fainted away. Doubtless Naters derived its name from this legend.

In the native State of Maisûr, in Southern India, snake worship appears to be now on the increase; it is believed to have existed there in very ancient times, to have died out, and then arisen again.

In support of this theory is the fact that hardly any traces of it are to be found amongst the rich sculptures which adorn the old temples at Bêlûr and Halêbîd in that state, also that all the Nâga sculptures we now see appear to be comparatively modern work. The only signs of snake worship in the temple at Bêlûr (which belongs to the Vaishnava sect, and has no snake emblems on the actual building) are two serpents of very inferior modern work carved upon a stone in the courtyard. At Halêbîd also the snake is only found in subordinate positions on the so-called twin temples at that place, which belong to the Śaiva sect—viz., on the stylobate of a porch where the gods are represented churning the sea with a large snake to serve as a rope for obtaining the *Amrita*. It is also to be seen on one of the exterior bands of sculpture, where Śiva is represented holding a Nâga Mûdamma on his left arm.[1]

In Bangalor, and in other places in the Maisûr State, the Nâga Mûdamma seems to be regarded as a sort of

[1] The Nâga Mûdamma is represented with the bust of a woman, the lower extremities that of a serpent or a fish-like tail.

tutelary saint.   At the entrance to every village there may commonly be seen a high pedestal, on which are fixed three upright slabs of gneiss (see Plate XV, figs. 3, 4, 5). On the centre slab is sculptured the Nâga lady, on the others the five or the seven-headed Nâga, and two serpents entwined as in the well-known *caduceus* of (Hermês) Mercury.

The late General Sir Alexander Cunningham, in the Preface to his *Bhilsa Topes*, identifies this latter form with the Buddhist symbol of *dharma*, identifying it with nature deified.   Again, some of the sculptures from the Buddhist remains at Amarâvatî, now in the British Museum, represent topes in miniature carved upon slabs.   They are covered with bas-reliefs.   The principal object on many of them is the five-headed serpent, the centre one being the hooded cobra in full face, and on either side two snakes' heads and necks.   In profile these seem to be regarding (or adoring?) the cobra.   The whole five heads terminate in one body, knotted into graceful folds.

From the style of the Maisûr carvings, it is thought that none of the Nâga Mûdamma sculptures are more than a century old.   It is well known that only within this period the people of the State have openly returned to their old forms of tree and serpent-worship, suppressed for many centuries, it is said, by Brahmanical influence, although in the head-dress now worn by the wives of Brahmans there, one may still trace (as in the case of the women of Ladakh) the influence of ancient-snake worship.   The women of that caste in Maisûr wear a lovely embossed gold ornament on the head. It descends only to the nape of the neck behind : it is wide in proportion to its length, and represents the many-headed

Nâga or cobra, frequently seen on Indian sculptures, with five, seven, nine, or more heads. Specimens of this snake ornament may be seen in the Indian Department of the South Kensington Museum.

Certain Indian families assert that they possess immunity from snake-bite. General (afterwards Sir William) Sleeman, in his *Journey through the Kingdom of Oudh*, mentions having been told by the Râjâ Tilokchand (whose family had settled themselves in that State) that no member of the family had ever been known to die from the effects of snake-bite. He accounted for this by saying that they were descended from *Sâlbâhan*, the rival and conqueror of Bikramâjît of Ujjain. Sâlbâhan is fabled to have been a lineal descendant of the snake god : he was most probably one of the leaders of the Scythian armies, who conquered India in the reign of Vikramâditya in Mâlwâ. The symbols of the snake woman are by no means confined to Asia. On Plate XVI, fig. 7, is a talisman called *La Sirena*, in use amongst the lower classes at Naples at the present day. I submit that a strong and decided family likeness exists between the Tartar goddess (Plate XV, fig. 1), the Nâga lady from Oudh, the Nâga Mûdammâ of Maisûr, Kiya Lûmê of Japan, and La Sirena of Naples, and that these all had most probably a common origin in the remote past. The Romans, too, would appear to have adopted into their symbolism a figure with a female bust, its lower extremity being that of a fish or a serpent. The object in the hand of the Tartar goddess has been by some supposed to denote the connection of this type of figure with Śaiva worship. It bears no very remote resemblance to one of the emblems of that god. A new light, however, would appear to have been thrown upon it by Japanese symbolic art. In a paper on *Netsukes*, by Mr Mortimer Mempes (*Magazine of Art*, 1889), is an illustration of a snake goddess, accompanied by the following legend :—High up, overlooking Lake Buva in Japan, stands the monastery of Mi-i-deva. There was a village beauty called Kiya Lûmê. Anchin, her admirer, was a priest of Mi-i-deva. After a time he bestowed his attentions on another lady ; he forsook Kiya Lûmê, and she in her rage and disappointment applied to the spirits of evil, entreating them to give her power to avenge herself on the perfidious Anchin. They granted her request, enabling her to take at will the form of a dragon. Assuming this shape, she went straight to the monastery where Anchin lived : he, fearing impending evil, had hidden himself under the great bell which was the fame and the pride of the monastery. Kiya Lûmê soon discovered his hiding-place, and coiling her snake-like tail round the bell, proceeded to hammer it until it melted by the heat generated by her repeated blows ; thus both Kiya Lûmê and Anchin perished together in the mass of molten metal.

The fancied resemblance of some natural objects, such as a mountain, a rock, or a grassy mound, to animals or other things which the natives of India venerate or hold sacred, has caused them to give simple names to certain spots, as, for instance, a small lake in Kashmir is called Nil nâg, and an alp or mountain pasture Nâg marg. Again Nâg kanda, or the shoulder of the snake, is the name given to a grassy knoll about thirty miles north of Simla. Nature, assisted possibly by art, has given this a likeness to a coiled snake.

The bushes near are profusely decorated with scraps of red material and other rags, the offerings of pilgrims. On the road to Kulu, not very far from this, is a hill of considerable height called Kanda Gai, or the shoulder of the cow. When viewed from a particular point, this eminence bears a strong resemblance to the humped variety of the bovine race.

On the whole, snake worship does not seem to have taken much hold on the minds of people living on the Continent of Europe : the reason probably being that snake worship, essentially a worship of fear, would naturally die out where the worst kinds of venomous snakes did not exist.

We will now proceed to give some instances of its survival in various countries, as regards certain actual beliefs, traditions, legends, customs, and sculptures bearing upon this subject.

A singular festival is still held once a year in Italy in a mountain village in the Abruzzi. On a certain day the peasants walk in procession, carrying round their arms, waists, and necks all the snakes they can find. They observe this custom in the belief that they will thus be secured from poison and from sudden death, and, further, that it will bring them good fortune, especially in love.

Numerous Roman coins and other objects have been found near Bielle and Arudy in the Basses Pyrenees. In the church at Laruns, near the Vallée D'Ossau, is a very singular white marble bénitier or stoup for holy water. It seems highly probable that this vessel was brought originally from one of the above-named places—Bielle, perhaps —since it is said that the remains of a Roman villa and of a splendid mosaic have been found there.

Tradition says that this vessel was discovered and put

to a religious use during the middle ages, at which time most likely the exterior decoration and the Christian symbol were added. The basin is circular, from twenty-seven to thirty inches in diameter. At the bottom of the interior is sculptured a fish, about ten inches in length, with back fin erect as if moving through the water. Round the inside of the vessel, at equal distances apart, and sculptured in high relief, are representations of a smaller fish, of a female figure terminating in the tail of a fish : she holds her tail in her left hand, and a small fish in her right. In addition to these is a centaur—half man and half horse ; its prototype we find in the Gandharvas of Indian mythology. In this instance the animal is represented galloping away from the Nâga goddess. The human or upper part of this figure is turned completely round ; with his cross-bow he seems to be aiming a flying shot at her. On the exterior of the basin is a band of raised geometric work, and an entwined monogram of the I H S in Gothic letters, both evidently fifteenth century work.

A good many of the legends of the Basque districts in the South of France turn upon a seven-headed serpent. Thus, the "Heren Suge" is always represented as being seven-headed, and in the myth of the "Serpent D'Isabit," the oldest version of the numerous tales of this nature, the serpent is fabled as lying with its head resting on the Pic du midi de Bigorre, its neck stretched towards Barèges, whilst its body fills the valley of Lùz, and its tail lies coiled in a hollow below the Cirque de Gavarnic.[1]

[1] Compare the Sub-Himâlayan legends about the demon Jâlandhara, the various parts of whose body occupy the country from Jalandhar to Kângra, a distance of one hundred and ten miles.

The Nâga lady again appears on the exterior of an oriel window of a corner house in one of the principal streets of Freiburg in Breisgau, in the Grand Duchy of Baden. On it are some interesting sculptured panels (presumably Roman work). The subject of the first, starting from the left, is a boy leading a hound by a leash; on the centre panel is a unicorn advancing rapidly towards a reclining female figure; immediately beneath this is a crowned female figure, the lower part of the body terminating in two tails, one held in each hand, as in "La Sirena" of Naples. On the extreme right is a male syren, also crowned, and ending in a fish with a divided tail, which he holds with each hand. The female figure has long flowing hair ; the male syren is represented with wings.

The inhabitants of the so-called Etsch That in South Tyrol (a district watered by the Adige) deem it a lucky circumstance to come across a certain species of snake. They say that many snakes have red heads, but the rest of their bodies are snow-white. These they style " Königs Wurmer " (or King's worms), adding that this kind is rarely found alone, but are generally accompanied by others—*black* snakes, and that whoever has the good fortune to see a King's worm may expect great happiness.

Switzerland also possesses a good many serpent legends. In a little work published at Lausanne, entitled *Légendes de la Suisse Romande*, a curious fact is cited—viz., that at the two extremities of the valley of Visp or Viège, that is to say, at Zermatt and at Saas, there are no snakes. The last one meets with are at Hoch Steg in the western valley, a bridge on this side of Zermatt, on the old bridle road between St Nicklaus and that place, and near Biderbach in the Saas valley on the eastern flank of the mountain. It is said that the people of Saas have tried to introduce them within these limits, but without success—the reptiles either perished at once like fish removed from their natural element, or else they went back in the direction from which they had been brought. The inhabitants of both Zermatt and Saas have their legends on this subject. A few years ago, when travelling through the Canton of Fribourg, the writer was told the following curious tale by an old peasant woman living in a small town which lies high up in the hills off the high road. This woman was probably over sixty years of age. Her story, as near as possible, ran thus : " A good many years ago (it was certainly before 1847, for the Jesuits were expelled in that year from their monastery near Fribourg), the people living near the Lac Noir in that canton were much troubled with the number of snakes or demons which infested that district. Yes, they were either snakes or demons, I know not which, but it is all the same. At last one of these Jesuit fathers went to the spot and exorcised them, so that they are all now in that lake, they cannot escape. I am quite sure that this is true," she added, with great emphasis.

In England, hazel and ash switches are looked upon by the people of Dartmoor in Devonshire as fit rods for charms. The natives of that district still believe that an ash stick is a protection against adders, which swarm on the moor, and that if a circle be made upon the ground with an ash stick, it will secure a serpent within it, also that if a fire be kindled within this charmed space, the creature would rather go into the fire than pass out of the circle.

In Scandinavia, remains of serpent-worship of a somewhat different signification are numerous; besides the Sun symbols which have been already described, there are certain other forms, such as the two-headed snake beneath the wheel (the wheel of the Sun ?) figured on Plate I, fig. 17. The late Kamer Herr Dr Worsaae[1] had come to the conclusion that these represent the Sun snake.[2] This seems to be confirmed by a reference to Plate V, fig. 15, which, as explained in Chapter III., is a sketch of a bronze fibula found a few years ago when excavating a Roman camp not far from Frankfort-on-the-Main. This little object would appear to show the connection between the *triskele* and the serpent. Each limb of the *triskele* has a serpent's head. The above-named learned professor, in his work on Danish Art, says : " The snake, as is well known, played an important part in the Asiatic and in the ancient Egyptian symbolism, partly because it was thought that the Sun's path through the heavens formed a curve like a snake, and partly because lightning, or the fertilising fire, flashed upon the earth in a snake-like zig-zag." From this " he concludes that the *triskele* was but an outcome or variety of the *Svastika*."

---

[1] Archæological science in Denmark, and, indeed, archæology in general, could hardly have sustained a greater loss than in the death of this distinguished professor in the full zenith of his powers. He was ever in the foremost rank of the discoverers of prehistoric remains in his own country, and, as in the case above cited, he seemed to be endowed with a power of grasping a subject, and of arriving at conclusions which were not apparent to others.

[2] Dr Schwartz of Berlin affirms from deep research into Greek and Roman mythology, that the paramount germinal idea in this widespread serpent emblem is the lightning, and Dr Brinton also gives the same opinion at some length.

CHAPTER X

THE EVIL EYE, AND ALLIED NOTIONS

ACCORDING to an old Hindû legend connected with Ganeśa
—the elephant-headed god—the son of Śiva and his wife
Pârvatî, as soon as he was born his parents invited all
the other gods and goddesses to come and see him, but by
an unlucky accident they omitted or forgot to invite Śani
(Saturn), who appeared on the scene in a terrible rage, and
with one glance of his eye caused the child's head to drop
off. The other gods, seeing what had happened, rushed out
in horror, and in their despair cut off the head of an elephant
which they found sleeping with her head towards the north.
This they clapt on to the infant's body, before its mother had
time to see and prevent the transformation.

This belief in the ill effects of the Evil Eye is fully held
in India at the present day. The modern Hindûstanî word
nazar, for a mischief glance, is not quite equivalent to the
English expression, " The Evil Eye " : it is much more comprehensive ; it implies the ill effects which may result from the
gaze of *any one*—even the most benevolent and affectionately
disposed, if that gaze has induced perfect satisfaction with
the object observed, whether animate or inanimate. Evil
intention is here left out of the question. It is for this reason
that Hindû mothers do not like any one—Europeans in particular—to admire their little ones too openly, nor to look at

138

them when they are eating, lest they should cast the Evil Eye on them. Amongst other methods of counteracting *nazar*, I may mention that in Calcutta the natives hold that a portion of all the food they buy in the market should be thrown into the fire to avert the Evil Eye. Muhammedans, too, are said to be, if possible, more fearful about *nazar* than Hindûs, and often to furnish these latter with texts from the *Qurân* to be used as amulets, in order to keep it off. In India, black or dark blue colours are frequently considered protective against *nazar*. Thus, in Upper Kunâwar, in the Satlaj valley, it is quite a common occurrence—I may say almost the usual thing—for a mother each morning to make a black mark on her infant's forehead and nose with a bit of burnt stick in order to preserve it from evil influence during the day. Once, too, after myself discarding some black dress material, I observed that our servants (who were all Pan-jâbis) had each taken a strip of it, and disposed it in some way about his turban or his dress, doubtless with this same idea.

On the above-mentioned principle, if a man be blind of one eye, or has any physical defect, he is believed to be likely to cast *nazar*, should he meet any one with a particularly fine pair of eyes ; and for this reason, many of the natives of India are said to put *kâjal* or lamp-black on their eyelids, or to have a piece of white thread hanging down from their turban or dress—anything, in short, to distract the attention of others, and avoid causing feelings of covetousness to arise in their minds. They also hold that if a person's eyes are en-circled with *kâjal* they are themselves incapable of casting *nazar*, and deem it a pretty thing for a woman thus to adorn herself, for in this case she can neither receive the ill effects of *nazar* nor impart it to others.

The custom of using colours to distract attention from the thing to be protected is not confined to black and blue alone. In various parts of India one sees all kinds of strange things painted in gaudy colours on the exterior of many of the houses, so that should any unlucky glance fall upon any dwelling it may be attracted to, and rest upon these representations, rather than on the house and its inmates. Similarly we find Madame Carla Serena in her interesting work, *Seule dans les Steppes* (which appeared in 1883), saying "that the Kirghiz have a great fear of the Evil Eye, and ornament the heads of their beasts of burden with bright-coloured ribbons to frighten it away." She speaks of having seen in her wanderings whole troops of camels thus decorated.

This same idea regarding *nazar* would seem to be not unknown in the British Isles, nor is it confined to the lower classes only. A Highland Minister's wife, when one of her children was much admired by a visitor, said to my informant after her guest's departure, "Oh dear, something is sure to happen to that child; I hope she has not given it the Evil Eye!" This same Scotch lady when starting for a country walk saw a hare cross the road, and nothing would induce her to proceed; she turned back, believing this to be a bad omen. We have already pointed out that the English idea of the Evil Eye differs somewhat from the Hindû notions regarding *nazar*.

The English peasantry in some counties still believe in so-called "Lucky Stones," *i.e.* self-bored ones. A correspondent of the English *Notes and Queries* relates, how, on entering a house in a Yorkshire village, he observed a ponderous necklace of such stones hanging against the wall. On enquiring about them, he found the good woman of the house at first indisposed to give him any information regarding them ; but he presently elicited from her that such stones had the credit of preserving the house and its inhabitants from the Evil Eye. " But," said he, "surely you don't believe in witches now-a-days ? " " No," she replied, " I don't say 'at I do, but certainly in former times there was wizards and hizzards, and them sort o' things." " Well," the gentleman rejoined, "but surely you don't think there are any now ? " " No, I don't say 'at there are, but I do believe in a Yevil Eye ! "

In India, diviners are called *Bhagats* or devotees, or *siyânâ*—wise men, they are supposed to work under the inspiration of a snake god. The power of divination is generally confined to the lower and menial (aboriginal?) castes, is often hereditary, and is rarely possessed by women. Inspiration is shown by the man's head beginning to wag, he then builds a shrine to his familiar, before which he dances, or as it is called by the people—sports. He is consulted at night, the enquirer providing tobacco and music. The tobacco is waved over the body of the invalid whom he has been called to attend, and given to the wise man to smoke. A lamp filled with *ghi* or clarified butter is then lighted, and the music plays. The diviner sometimes lashes himself with a whip : at length he is seized with the afflatus, and in a paroxysm of dancing and head wagging, he declares the name of the malignant influence, the manner in which it is to be propitiated, and the time when the disease may be expected to abate. The diviner waves wheat over the patient's body ; (Saturday or Sunday are the days preferred for these ceremonies) he then counts out the grains one by one into heaps, one heap for each god who is likely to be at the bottom of the mischief, and the deity on whose heap the last grain falls is the one to be propitiated. The malignant spirit has to be appeased by building for him a new shrine, or by making offerings at the old one. Very often the offering is first placed on the patient's head for a night, or waved over his body, or he is made to eat a portion of it ; it is also sometimes exposed on a moonlight night, when the moon is on the increase, together with a lighted lamp, at a place where four cross roads meet. Sometimes it is thought sufficient to tie a rag taken from the patient's body on a sacred tree, generally a *Jhand* (*prosopis spicigera*) beneath which the shrine stands : such trees may often be seen covered with the remnants of those offerings, *blue* being the predominating colour if the shrine be Musalmân, and *red* if it be Hindû.

A singular development of the idea that trees which have natural excrescences in the shape of nails are a protection against evil spirits generally, rather than against the Evil Eye only, came under our notice when travelling in the Maisûr State. A European Government official chanced to be making a tour of inspection through that particular district. As is usual, a number of natives came to him every day, some with wrongs to be redressed, and others simply to pay their respects to him. In this latter category was an old native who had served in the late Mahârâjâ's bodyguard. On this important occasion he wore his former uniform, abundantly ornamented with gold lace. In his right hand he held a stick of colossal proportions,—its upper part was as thick as a man's arm, the lower end about the size of a man's wrist: to it were attached many silver rings and knobs. It was made from a branch of the *Bombax Malabaricum* (*Simal*), a tree common to the jungles thereabouts, it produces pods which, when ripe, contain a mass of silky golden-coloured cotton fibre; both the trunk and the branches of this tree are thickly studded with protuberances which resemble *blunt* nails. When asked why he carried such a formidable looking stick, the old man replied :— " Furnished with such a stick as this, any one can walk safely at night through the jungles without fear of demons." He thus evidently did not carry it to protect him against ill disposed persons, but to guard him against the spirits of evil.

In the Western Himâlayas, on the left bank of the Satlaj river, is an oasis called Pû, which at a rough guess is about three miles in circumference. It is about a day's march from Shipki, in Chinese Tibet, a country from which Europeans have been rigidly excluded since the early part of the present century. Pû is situated at a height of 9400 feet above sea level ; it is a lovely green oasis covered with apricot trees and surrounded by bare and rocky mountains, and in such an out of the way spot that it is not even marked on Montgomerie's map, nor is it named in the list of Himâlayan routes. Immediately opposite Pû, on the other side of the river, is a high, rugged mountain regarding which—as a German missionary who had resided there seventeen years told us—more than one native had related to him how that in former days— no one seemed to know exactly how long ago—this mountain was the abode of an evil spirit, which from time to time took the form of a scorpion ; it was as large as a goat, entered villages, seized and devoured children and cattle. At length, so the tale runs, a Lama or Buddhist monk came from a great distance and banished the bad spirit to a cleft in this mountain. In order to propitiate him, it was customary every year to sacrifice a boy of eight years old and a young calf; this was done by throwing them down alive into this cleft. This barbarous custom ceased, they say, ever since a second Lama came, who was able entirely to destroy the demon's power.

In certain parts of Greece, if a child be admired, it causes the mother the greatest consternation ; thus, Greek mothers frequently decorate their infants' caps with coins or other bright ornaments, in order to divert attention from the child to these objects. Any expression of approval or of admiration is met with the entreaty, " Don't give it the evil eye," and the mother immediately points with two fingers at the person in question, accompanying the gesture with the Greek word for *Garlic*, which is deemed a sovereign remedy against this malign power. The origin of this notion is probably to be found in an idea, prevalent both in parts of India and in Spain, that garlic and onions are preservatives against fever.[1]

In Smyrna the notion exists that the Evil Eye is inherent in certain people ; the lower classes deem it very unlucky to be looked at by anyone with grey eyes. When in Corfu in 1883, I met with a combination of the above notions in one

[1] The natives of Sweden, if they happen to meet anyone who is afflicted with any grievous disorder, at once exclaim Pepper ! thinking by this means to avert any evil consequences from themselves.

individual, viz., a Christian woman from Alexandria, whose
nationality was doubtful; she spoke Italian fairly well, but I
fancy she had a mixture of European and Egyptian blood in
her veins. An infant about eight months old was in 'her
arms; its waist was encircled with several strings of coral, to
which were attached a silver whistle and bells, a boar's tusk,
coral charms like those in use at Naples against the Evil
Eye, a piece of mother-o'-pearl set in silver—the image of
some saint was engraved upon it,—and a small silk bag. I
ascertained on enquiry that this bag contained some salt,
a piece of charcoal, a nail, and a clove of garlic. Lastly, on
the centre of the child's forehead was an object resembling a
dark blue wafer, which the mother said was to keep off the
Evil Eye. The connection of these objects with Asiatic and
European superstitions is obvious.

In South Tyrol the people say that when driving at night
the whip should be cracked very freely, in order to scare away
ghosts and witches. They are also in the habit of making
a crooked cross upon their flour and corn, and upon freshly
churned butter, in order, as they say, to drive away evil
spirits. The Irish, also, hold a somewhat similar superstition.
In the South of Ireland, more especially in County Cork, no
woman belonging to the lower classes will put a hen to sit
upon a clutch of eggs without having previously, with a
charred stick, marked each egg with the sign of the cross.
Were this omitted, they firmly believe the eggs would come
to nought.

The Tyrolese hold many other singular superstitions.
High up in the hills, between Meran and Botzen, is a large
reddish-coloured patch of land, which looks like a freshly-

ploughed field. That they call the Sunday acre ; it is unfruitful. It belonged at one time to a peasant, who, notwithstanding the warnings of the priest, would work his land on Sundays. One harvest-time his entire crop disappeared, and since then it has never been possible to grow anything in that field. The peasants, even now, are wont to point out this spot to their children, saying : " See ! up there is the Sunday acre, the fruit of Sunday work." Another legend they have is, that when Eve was somewhat old, God asked her how many children she had had. Not exactly remembering, she gave a number 2000 or 3000 too few, and in consequence these latter became bewitched men—apes—and it is still believed there that apes are exiled men. What would Darwin have said to this theory ?

The Tyrolese also hold that whoever sees a four-leaved clover has much happiness in store for him ; but he should not pluck it, for the rhyme says :—

" *Selig das Auge das ihm sieht,*
Verflucht die Hand, die ism bricht."

" Blessed is the eye which sees it,
Cursed is the hand that plucks it."

They say that teeth which have fallen out should be placed in a wall, or where they can most easily be found at the day of judgment, for then all the parts of the body must be collected together. Again, when it thunders, these people say—

" Der Herr Gott leert steine ab."

(" God is clearing away stones.")

Another saying is : " Silk-worms, bees, and ants are the servants of the Church—viz., silk, wax, and incense."

In Savoy it is the belief of the people that a funeral should not take place on a Monday or a Friday, for it brings misfortune ; there would be another death in the same house within the year, should the cross (as carried in funeral processions) enter the house on either of these days.

We will now turn our attention to certain amulets in use at Naples in the present day. They appear to serve in some degree to connect the East and West. There seems but little doubt that many of the Neapolitan customs and super-stitions were brought thither by Greek colonists, who settled at Cumae and elsewhere, and whose ancestors again were possibly in very remote times some of the earliest wanderers from Central Asia into Europe. The Neapolitans, as we will proceed to show, approach Eastern types in many of their customs, as well as in certain features of their character. The higher classes are clever and acute, but they want tenacity of purpose ; they develop very early, but they lack accuracy and method in business matters, and in small things also ; whilst the lower classes are deeply imbued with superstitions of an Oriental kind.

In Naples the most common form of charm against the *jettatura* or evil eye is a tiny ornament resembling a bull's horn, made either of gold, silver, or coral. It is almost universally worn attached to the watch chain. It may possibly have originally had a threefold signification :—

1. As the horn of plenty, bringing good fortune.
2. As a protection against evil influences coming from without ; and

3. May not this little talisman have had originally some association with the idea of the scapegoat?

The following anecdote, related to the writer by an Italian lady who knew one of the parties concerned, would seem to indicate that this is not an impossible suggestion :— A family of her acquaintance had settled themselves down in an apartment in Naples. Shortly afterwards, another flat in the same house was taken by a lady whom the first comers believed possessed the Evil Eye. They were in despair at this, and in order to avert any bad consequences which might result to themselves from this circumstance, they caused a bull to be brought to the house, and had this animal driven through the entrance archway and round and round the courtyard for some hours.

This custom is in close connection with a well-known one in India. At the present day Hindûs are in the habit of turning kine loose to wander about, after some person's sins have been transferred to the animals by the performance of certain ceremonies. A somewhat analogous custom prevails in Gloucestershire. When anyone discovers that they possess what is commonly styled a crowing hen, the bird is immediately driven forth from the poultry-yard to a spot where three cross roads meet, and there left to wander whither it likes.

To give an instance of the further development of this idea in the East, we would observe that Dr Schuyler in his *Turkestân* speaks of a custom existing in that country, which is worth quoting in this connection. He says : " Life in Ach Kûrgân was rather dull : amusement there was none, all games being strictly forbidden. Such things as jugglery, dancing, and comic performances are, I am told, forbidden in the Khanate, the licentious Khân having seen the error of his ways, and having put on, for his people at least, the semblance of virtue. Of praying there was very little : occasionally in the afternoon or at sunset some few pious individuals would spread out a rug and make their supplications to Allah. One poor old man, however, I noticed, who seemed constantly engaged in prayer. On calling attention to him, I was told that he was an *iskachi*, a person who makes his living by taking upon himself the sins of the dead, and thenceforward devoting his life to prayer for their souls. He corresponds to the sin-eater of the Welsh border."

On Plate XVII are figured several forms of an amulet still in use at Naples. In all of these we find the tree, the serpent, an arm, a hand holding a horn (the horn of plenty?) within which is a half moon, the emblem of Janara or the Moon, also a key, the emblem of Janus or the Sun, who was fabled to have taught men to build houses and to close them with doors. (Janua) being also the Sun, it was considered suitable that he should have the keys of the doors of heaven, in order that he might open them at dawn and close them at sunset. Neapolitan women of the lower class are in the habit of making use of this word *Janara* (the Moon, the wife of Janus) as an epithet of reproach ; if angry with one of their own sex they will call her a *Janara*—a witch. It was only after some searching and many enquiries in the quarter of the town called Old Naples that these various forms of this talisman were obtained. At first, the people seemed ashamed to own that they held such a superstition, but after several visits and much ques-

tioning they were induced to tell their use and give, we
believe, the true name for these little silver ornaments, viz.:
cima-ruta, top or head of rue. It is there the custom to
strew sprigs of rue round the couch of a woman and her
newly born infant: the talisman itself is bound over the
heart of the child (thence most probably its name) in order
to protect it against evil influences. In the use of rue, we
have a distinct connection between the customs of the East
and West. In India, *rue* (*sudâb*) is used in various ways as
a charm against evil.[1] *Colebrooke* says, when describing a
native wedding in that country, "the bridegroom goes in
procession to the house of the bride's father and is there wel-
comed as a guest. The bride is given to him by her father
in the form usual at every solemn donation, and their hands
are bound together with grass. He clothes the bride with
an upper and better garment, the skirts of her mantle and of
his are tied together. The bridegroom makes an oblation
to fire and the bride drops *rue* upon it as an oblation."

This custom of tying together the garments of a bride and
bridegroom is also noted by Sir W. W. Hunter in his *Annals
of Rural Bengal*. Speaking of the Santhals, he says, "The
husband's clans-men knot together the dresses of the bride
and bridegroom as a sign that the woman by marrying quits
the clan and the gods of her father to adopt those of her
husband." Mr H. H. Bancroft, Vol. II. p. 257, relates that
an Astec bride knelt at her husband's left hand, and that
the dresses of the pair were tied together.

Again, Captain Bourke in his work on the *Moquis of
Arizona* gives the following account of a Moqui marriage,

---

[1] See Dymock's *Vegetable Mat. Med. of W. India*, 1st ed., p. 98.

which he had from an intelligent man, who had been left with those people as a child and had grown up amongst them :—
" Whilst the wedding guests were paying their respects to the feast set before them, the bride and the bridegroom retired to an inner room, disrobed, bathed themselves from head to foot in clear water. They then went back to the long room where the guests were assembled and were invested with new cotton garments, the ends of which were tied together." To bring this custom nearer home—it is stated in an account of a gipsy wedding which recently took place in a suburb of Vienna, that at one part of the ceremony an old man handed a yellow scarf to the Captain (who officiated as priest), and that the latter bound it round the wrists of the happy pair, saying as he did so, " man and wife must be bound together."

There is another curious circumstance in connection with marriage amongst some of these Indian tribes which is worthy of note. After marriage, a Moqui may speak to his mother-in-law and sit in the same room with her, but the Apaches and the Navajoes do not permit this. A somewhat similar notion prevails amongst the Arabs in North Africa ; we give it as an instance of the singular fact of like customs being found amongst peoples who are now widely separated in country, race, and religion.

Some few years ago, when visiting the Dhara, an isolated mountain district in North Africa, situated between the plain and the sea, and which was then only being opened out by the French, the author and her husband were for a couple of days the guests of the Kâïd or local native governor. His family consisted of himself, his wife, his son, a youth of sixteen, who had already been married two years to a girl who was a couple of years his junior, and a child of tender years. Father and son both spoke French well, the latter invited the writer to pay a visit to the Harem which was situated within a courtyard attached to the principal building and surrounded by a high wall. When thus introduced by this youth into the private apartments of his wife and mother, we made a nice *partie carrée*, he acting as interpreter. Suddenly, whilst we were talking, the door of the courtyard clicked, the young man jumped up in the middle of a sentence and went sideways out of the room *with his face to the door* as his father entered it, this, as I was afterwards informed, it was his imperative duty to do, since it would be highly improper that he should see his wife in the presence of his father. The young wife, who until then had sat with us as an equal, went to meet her father-in-law, kissed his hand, and then retreated into one corner of the room, standing there during the rest of the visit.

In Bengal, a somewhat similar idea prevails amongst the Brahmans, viz. : a woman is never permitted to see any of her husband's elder brothers ; the younger ones she may meet and converse with. Their marriages too, are subject to peculiar laws. It is the duty of a certain class of people, who may be styled walking peerages, to keep regular registers of Brahman families extending back for many past generations ; it is a rule with them that a man may only marry a woman of the same generation as himself, *e.g.*, should he be the twenty-fifth in the line of descent, his wife must be so also. It is likewise forbidden to them to marry any one having the same surname as themselves—though there may be no relationship between them.

After this somewhat long digression, we shall return to another portion of our subject—the use of *Rue*. In England this plant was anciently named " Herb Grace" or " Herb of Grace." Warburton says that this latter name was given to it from its being used in exorcisms. When a child, the writer well remembers having frequently observed a practice in one of our midland counties which was a possible survival of the idea of Rue as " Herb of Grace." It was then not uncommon to see many of the middle-aged and elderly labourers' wives walking to church with a sprig of Rue in their hands together with a prayer-book and a neatly folded handkerchief. With us still, the word Rue signifies repentance ; what then more natural (its original use having doubtless been forgotten) than that those who were about to join in a general confession of repentance should adopt its emblem?

As an instance of an idea existing long after any reasonable explanation of it has been forgotten, we may here mention that in many English villages the children are taught that they must not point at the stars, but are not told why it is wrong. In Germany, the same thing is inculcated, the reason there given for it is, that the stars are the angel's eyes. (Wolf, *Beitrage zur Deutschen Mythologie.*)

An even more beautiful idea was once, to the writer's knowledge, expressed by a little English girl, who after gazing long at the star-spangled firmament said, "I have found out what the stars are, they are holes which God makes in the sky, that we may see heaven through them."

In Burke's *Romance of the Forum* it is stated that during the trial of Mrs Manning the murderess, "the bench of the dock was, according to custom, strewn with rue." This practice was afterwards discontinued; at the Old Bailey, instead of herbs, a small bouquet of flowers was placed upon the Judge's desk from April to October. In *Notes and Queries* (London 1857), with reference to the use of rue at the Old Bailey, we read that in Laurence's *Life of Fielding* it is stated that this custom arose after a contagious disease which had been engendered by the foul atmosphere of that Court of Justice upwards of one hundred years previously, and in Bland's *Popular Antiquities* it is mentioned that in Aristotle's time rue was hung about the neck as an amulet against witchcraft.

This word "Witchcraft" strikes the keynote of another branch of our subject—the being bewitched or "overlooked," which is the more usual expression in the British Isles.

A few years ago, when in the Maisûr state, I was told of a native, aged about twenty-seven, a young man of education, and possessed of considerable talent, who then occupied a post of some importance under the Government. He was either the grandson or the great-grandson of Purnia, who was Regent and Prime Minister of Maisûr during the long minority of the Mahârâjâ, who was placed on the throne in 1799 by the British Government after the taking of Seringapatam. This young official, Krishna Murti by name, had a firm conviction that in consequence of a curse which had been placed upon all the male members of his family, many years previous to his birth, he would not survive his thirty-second year. Purnia is said to have been an excellent administrator; for some reason he caused one of his sons-in-law to be falsely accused of some crime, and afterwards executed. This man, before he was put to death, declared that no son, or son's son of his father-in-law's, would ever live to pass his then age—thirty-one. It was stated to us as a positive fact that, invariably since that time, the male members of that family have died before attaining that age. Most probably, the feeling that their doom was fixed has had its effect upon the minds of those persons, and thus contributed to the fulfilment of this prophecy.

A very peculiar race of people exists on the Island of Guernsey; they are accounted witches, and are thought to have the power of casting the Evil Eye. As far as I have hitherto been able to learn, nothing is positively known of their origin or their antecedents. Some have thought they might be a remnant of a Keltic population, others have imagined that they are of Spanish or of Gipsy blood. In type, features, and complexion they are totally different from the other inhabitants of that island; they have very black hair and eyes, and olive complexions. They are called " The Pipets" (plural, Pipiaux). These Pipiaux are all small farmers, they live chiefly in St Saviour's parish, in the district called the Forest, and near Lihou.

Some of the women occasionally go round to the different gentlemen's houses to dispose of their fowls, etc. Such is the dread which a visit from one of these people inspires in the mind of a true Guernsey servant, that should her mistress not purchase anything of them, she will herself bestow a small coin, and on their departure throw a handful of salt after them. Until very recently no true Guernsey man or woman would venture to marry a Pipet: a mixed marriage, however, did take place two or three years ago, and it is said the couple are living happily together in St Martin's Parish.

I was told that this union was looked upon at the time as tempting Providence. A curious anecdote of these people was related to me by a lady who belongs to one of the oldest families on that island. Before she married she resided in her father's house, situated about two miles from the town. It was not an unusual circumstance for some of the poorer Pipiaux to come to their door at Christmas time to ask for a present, and it was never refused them. One Christmas Day, a family who lived near them, not only would not give anything to a Pipet who came, but ordered the suppliant to go away, on which this latter said—"You think you are going to have a very good dinner to-day, but you are much mistaken."

The dinner hour came, the roast beef and the roast turkey had been some hours before the fire but they could not be cooked, and in despair they at length sent over to the house of my informant's father to beg for a dinner. The only rational solution of the mystery was that their larder, being in a cold situation, the meat had become frozen ; but no doubt the servants of both families preferred to adhere to the theory that the provisions had been bewitched.

A superstition which is allied to the Evil Eye still prevails in Guernsey—there called being " overlooked."

A few years ago a fine strong healthy girl, house and parlour-maid in a family of my acquaintance, was observed to become absent in her manner, neglectful in her duties, and to have a distraught look ; she would sit for hours together (contrary to her usual custom) with her hands folded in her lap.   On being questioned by her Mistress, the girl acknowledged that she was much disturbed in mind, because she was quite sure that a certain old woman who lived near, had "*overlooked*" her.   The lady reasoned with her, but in vain ; at length, the family medical man was consulted, he tried at first to laugh the girl out of her fancies but it was of no use, she got worse and worse ; on being taken to the Island of Sark she entirely recovered her normal health and spirits, but relapsed into her previous melancholy condition on returning to Guernsey.   In the end it was thought best that she should go out to some relations in America.   She is now married there and doing well.

The following tale was taken down in 1890-91 from the lips of a middle-aged English woman, whose parents settled in Guernsey when she was a child ; she herself seemed half to believe it, her mother (deceased two years before) evidently did so completely, but her father, then a very old man, scouted and still ridicules the idea of anyone having such a power of doing evil.   It is said that very old Guernsey peasant folk are very deeply embued with a belief in witch-craft and in being "overlooked," and that the young ones laugh at such things, but that when they in their turn reach the forties or fifties they are just as credulous as their for-bears.   But to my story :—

Mrs X., aged 44 years, was—when a child of ten, while seated at tea with her parents—suddenly taken with a kind of shaking fit, so violent was the attack that she knocked the things off the table ; it affected one side of her face and of her body only.   More than one doctor were consulted, but they could do nothing for her. At length—at the end of three years, her mother went to a reputed Witch doctor called Van Courtenay; his first question was, "Whether she (the mother) had any enemy?" On her replying in the affirmative, and telling him that the man she suspected of injuring her daughter was a Jersey-man, named Hammon, Van Courtenay said, that this man's mother was a well known witch. He gave some medicine for the child (which however her father would not allow her to take), at the same time saying that she would not get well until they took her over to England: they had already tried Sark: and that would break the spell. This singular illness left her as soon as she reached England, though she was very weak for some time afterwards.

The power attributed by these islanders to witches and wizards (they have both) is curious in some respects. They say it is dangerous to refuse such people anything, but it is possible to circumvent them, as was once done by a man whom Belier Bœuf, a notorious wizard, asked to stand god-father to his child. This person dared not give Belier a decided refusal; but he consented to be godfather on condition that the child should be called "Gigot de——" (Anglice-leg-of). The wizard could not make up his mind to have his son called "Gigot de——" before his patronymic name of Bœuf, so he let the man off Scot free, since under the circumstances he would be powerless to bewitch him. This story is true, but the name is fictitious; this reputed wizard was a well known character in his day, some of his descendants are possibly still living.

In Guernsey, within very recent times, the god-parents

had the privilege of bestowing any name they liked upon their god-children, and frequently the father and the mother would hear their child's name for the first time in church from the clergyman who baptized the babe.

In some parts of England also, the peasantry and even the small farmer class still believe in wizards and witches. In the village of Blakemere, situated about eleven miles from Hereford, and united to the parish of Preston on Wye, there was, two or three years ago, and probably is still, a young man who is said to be a "dangerous person"—which means that he is able by some supernatural power which he possesses, to injure anyone who offends him : in fact, he is accounted a wizard.

Devonshire people, more especially those living on and around Dartmoor, would seem to be firm believers in charms and witchcraft : such superstitions are firmly engrained in the minds of even small farmers and intelligent people above the peasant class. They have, however, discovered what they deem to be an effectual mode of counteracting the evil influence of the malignant or *black* witch; they employ for this purpose a class of men known as *white* wizards. Two such witch doctors reside in the city of Exeter, their fee is a guinea, they have a large *clientèle* amongst the farmers living on or near Dartmoor, a third lives at Launceston in Cornwall. These men were plying their trade as lately as 1888; they are said to use incantations and the planetary signs, but neither potions nor any other form of remedy. At Lydford, which is on the line of railway, there is less talk of witchcraft, but of charms without end ; for instance—one Peter Hill, sexton and parish clerk, professes to be able to staunch blood in men, women, children, and animals. He is himself subject to profuse bleedings at the nose, and declares that he can always stop it by using as an incantation the sixth verse of the sixteenth chapter of Ezekiel. He and others are firm believers in the efficacy of this charm, he says the knowledge of it can only be communicated by a man to a woman, or by a woman to a man. The postmaster too of that place, who was formerly a schoolmaster of the hedgerow kind, is believed to be able to remove warts by incantation; a young man assured my informant that he had cured him of several on his hands, also that another man's pony, which was much disfigured by warts on its nose, had been successfully treated by him. There was also in the same place a woman called Lane, who could cure white swellings on the knee, she had cured the postmaster of that disease. Lane asserts, as well as Peter Hill, that a woman may tell the charm to a man, but not to one of her own sex. Lane, it seems, merely requires to see the handkerchief (it must be a new one) with which the knee is to be bound; she repeats a formula over it each time it is removed from the patient's knee, this must be repeated seven times.

The landlady of the inn at Lydford is thought to be in possession of a stone of extraordinary virtue : its local name is the " Kanen Stone," it was picked up by her husband on the moor seventy years ago. This stone is accredited with the property of removing cataract or blood-shot from the eyes. It is said to be about the size of a cherry, and to look like a piece of white agate ; on one side is a cloudy mark beneath the surface, and on the other a red mark like blood. When using it the afflicted person must stand facing the sun, and strike his eye with the stone three times, each time drawing it across his eye between the lids "the way of the Sun." This ceremony must be performed in the early morning : the operation should be three times repeated. The same plan is adopted for blood-shot eyes : the coloured side of the stone is then used.

The natives of the moor have also their unlucky days, they deem the third Sunday after Christmas (Cross-day as they term it) an unlucky one : they will neither marry nor begin any enterprise on that day.

We have already spoken of Blakemere in Herefordshire in connection with witchcraft ; we shall now mention some of the charms which are still in use in that parish and in other parts of that county. Once, when there was an epidemic of whooping-cough in the place, an old woman said to the rector ; " Lor! bless you, sir, when I was a girl we thought nothing of it, we never troubled the doctor. The child was taken to the mill, the miller set the mill going and said, ' In the name of the Father, the Son, and the Holy Ghost, I grind away this disease,' and it always went—always." She added that to wear an offertory shilling, *i.e.*, a coin collected at the offertory during the celebration of Holy Communion, is also regarded as a charm against the attacks of certain diseases, or in some cases, as a cure for them. The rector also stated that he has been frequently asked for a coin for this purpose.

The same notion prevails in the Tyrol. The people say that one should always carry a consecrated kreutzer (the smallest coin they have) in the purse, in order that the other money may not be quickly spent.

At Bredwardine, and several other places in Hereford-shire, it is the custom for many of the villagers to bake a special batch of bread on Good Friday, not every year perhaps, but as occasion requires. Tiny loaves of this bread are preserved with great care, and used for the common ailments which flesh is heir to. This bread is sometimes ground to powder, mixed with hot water, or some other liquid, and taken as a medicine. They firmly believe that bread baked on that day has a special virtue in it, which prevents it from ever getting mouldy. The legend which they connect with it is a curious and interesting one. It runs thus : " As our Blessed Lord was carrying his cross on his way to his crucifixion, a woman who had been washing, came out of her house and threw her dirty water over the Saviour ; another woman who was standing near with some freshly baked bread, said to her; 'Why do you treat that poor man like that, one who never did you any harm ?' and she gave our Blessed Lord a loaf which He ate and said, ' From henceforth blessed be the baker, and cursed be the washer.' "

In Gloucestershire too, the older people have a superstition that if they wash and hang out their linen to dry on Good Friday, they will find it spotted with blood when they take it in.

Both in Herefordshire and in Guernsey, women of the servant class deem it very unlucky to turn the mattresses of a bed on a Friday ; possibly the same notion exists in other parts of England also. A Guernsey girl gave as a reason : " Because Friday is the witches' day, on it they hold their so-called *Sabbat* or general meeting (this idea prevails both in Guernsey and in France), and should the mattresses be turned, it is quite certain that some of the wicked creatures would get in between them, and give the occupier of that bed a most uneasy night."

From witches and wizards it is an easy transition to soothsayers and diviners. Both in India and in Europe diviners are consulted when any article has been stolen, in order that the thief may be discovered.

In India, when a diviner is sent for, he brings with him two assistants; he is provided with a pair of scissors, some rice, and a sieve, such as is there used for winnowing grain. Both the sieve and the scissors have in this case a very significant meaning; the sieve is considered emblematical of the rain clouds, and in many lands iron is deemed an effectual charm against evil spirits. When the charm is about to be tried, a fire is lighted in an earthen pot, the diviner takes up the winnowing vessel (made of a kind of basket work), its edges are bent up on three sides, the fourth side is flat. After having stuck the scissors into the upper and deepest edge of the sieve, and having repeated certain prayers and incantations, he causes his two assistants each to put a finger beneath the holes of the scissors; and in this manner they hold the sieve suspended over the fire. All the inmates of the house, whose owner has desired his presence, must then, each in turn, take a small quantity of uncooked rice in their hands and drop the grains into the flames through the fork formed by the open scissors— the diviner all the while repeating certain formulas. All goes on very smoothly until the guilty person attempts to scatter his rice; the grain sifter in that case begins to turn round rapidly, and thus the true culprit is exposed. An English lady who saw this method employed in Bangalor by her own servants, said that the test was, in that instance, perfectly successful, and the guilty one—a woman—seeing that her theft had thus been discovered, confessed to having stolen a rug from a fellow-servant.

Brockett, in his Glossary of English North Country words, cites a parallel custom. "The vulgar in many parts," he says, "have an abominable practice of using a riddle and a pair of scissors in divination. If they have had anything stolen from them, the riddle and the shears are sure to be resorted to."

Another development of this idea is to be found in Northumberland, where girls are said to turn a riddle in order to raise their lovers. A similar mode of discovering thieves, or detecting the guilt of a person accused of any crime, prevailed amongst the Greeks.

Herefordshire also had, and possibly has still, its diviners. Not so very long ago, one resided in Bredwardine; he is now dead, and I have been unable to ascertain whether his mantle is supposed to have fallen upon anyone else. The parish clerk of that place, when asked about such people, related the following story :—

"Some sixty or seventy years ago a farmer's wife belonging to Bredwardine stole the parson's surplice out of the church, in order to spite some of the singers ; at the same time she spread a report that one of them was the culprit. They were naturally much annoyed and tried to find out the thief, but all to no purpose. At last, hearing that there was a wizard living at Preston-on-Wye, one of their number went to consult him and told him all their troubles and difficulties. When asked if he could discover the thief, the diviner said, ' Would you know him if I show him to you?' 'Certainly,' was the reply, 'if he belongs to Bredwardine.' Upon this the diviner consulted his books, and after a while the form of a woman appeared whom his visitor at once recognised as the wife of a farmer at Bredwardine. He returned home, went to this farmer's house, and taxed the woman with the theft. She did not deny it, but going to a cupboard in the room, produced the surplice and handed it over to him, much to his satisfaction and also to that of the other singers, who were thus relieved from the unjust accusation which had been hanging over them."

I will here give one or two more instances in which customs of a closely allied form are found in India and in Europe. Many wandering native traders in India who sell shawls, stuffs, cloths, calicoes, etc., are in the habit of coming into the verandahs of the European banglows to dispose of their goods. Should any article purchased of them be the first thing they have sold that day, they will, on receiving their money, take the rupees one by one, and with the coins touch first their forehead, their mouth, and, lastly, their yard measure.

A somewhat similar proceeding is in use in Guernsey. Chancing to go into an old curiosity shop, a cart arrived with a load of goods which had been bought the day before ; investing in some of these articles, I paid for them in five franc pieces. The shop-keeper, a woman, spat upon one or more of the coins, apologising for doing so, saying that it was for luck, these things being the first she had sold out of that consignment. In London this practice is confined to beggars and street vendors.

We would here draw attention to a singular custom still existing in Guernsey called *Le Clameur du Haro*; it is probably known to but few persons out of the island. It is not recorded whether this curious custom was instituted by the famous Rollo himself, or whether it took its rise among the people, owing to their extreme reverence for the justice of his laws and decrees.[1]

Le Clameur du Haro is used when a man finds another in any way encroaching upon his property or possessions; he goes to the spot accompanied by witnesses, and in their presence he makes a declaration against such proceedings, crying out three several times, " Ha! Ro!" and in the King's (Queen's) name discharges any workmen whom he may find upon the place, after which he applies either to the Bailiff or to his Lieutenant, or in their absence to two of the Jurats of the Royal Court, and says what he has done. The proceedings are then registered at the Greffier's office and the plaintiff commences an action in the Court. If he does not do so, the person against whom he has cried Ha! Ro! may become the plaintiff in the suit. Upon the action of one or other of the parties, the Court proceeds to give its decision, and whichever (either plaintiff or defendant) is condemned, he is fined to the King eighteen sols, and *un regard*

---

[1] " Whether," as Dr Shebbe says in his *History oj Jersey*, " it sprung from the just discernment of Rollo, or was derived from a like custom among the Sauronates, from whom the Romans might have been originally descended, is not to be determined ; it was a usage not confined to these nations. The Greeks in similar cases invoked the name of Hercules, the Egyptians of Isis, the Romans of their Emperors, and the Jews of their good king Ezechias."

de Chateau, or twenty-four hours' imprisonment, and to pay all costs. Thus, to implore the aid of the Prince when there is no just cause, and the disturbing of the public peace by invading another's property, are accounted equally criminal.[1]

Falle, the historian, relates a curious anecdote regarding the virtue and power of this formula, which occurred about 170 years after Rollo's decease, when the burial of William the Conqueror's body was opposed by a subject. It seems that in order to build the great Abbey of St Stephen at Caen, where the king intended his body should lie, William the Conqueror had caused several houses to be pulled down to enlarge the area. Amongst these there was one for which the owner had received no compensation. Some say that the son of the owner—others that this person himself— observing that the grave had been dug on the very spot where his house before stood, came boldly into the Assembly and forbade them (not in the name of God, but in Rollo's name) to bury the body there.

Coote, in his *History of England,* tells us that the name of the owner was Fitz-Arthur, and that a small sum was paid him on the spot for the right of immediate burial, and that Prince Henry afterwards gave him full satisfaction for the rest of his claim. A very few years ago the force of this ancient appeal was tested and acknowledged in Guernsey. Fifty years ago—possibly still more recently—a wooden cage stood in the Guernsey market-place. People were confined

[1] The exact words used are " Ha-Ro ! three times repeated, and *A mon aide Mon Prince ! On me fait tort ! Ha* is an exclamation of suffering or distress, and *Ro* is an abbreviation of Duke Rollo's name, so that this is as much as to say : O ! Rollo, my Prince, succour me ! "

in it for some hours for petty thefts or drunkenness, exposed to the gibes and jeers of the populace.

Sir Edgar MacCulloch, the late Bailiff of Guernsey, told the writer that it was at one time the custom that a woman accused of concealing the birth of her child should stand at the bar of the Royal Court, when the Bailiff and the Jurats were sitting, clad in a white sheet, and there acknowledge her fault.

The natives of Guernsey also hold that one must not look into a well on Christmas night, because the water is turned into wine ; neither should one enter a cow stall, because the cattle are then on their knees. The same idea is current at a place called Neudorf, near Schassburg, in Transylvania, where there is a prevalent superstition that at midnight on New Year's night the cattle speak, but in a language which man may not hear. Should he do so his life is the forfeit.

Another remarkable superstition survives both in India and in Europe. The custom is cited in *Panjab Notes and Queries*, Vol. I, note 219, according to which, if a married couple have lost several male children, and a boy is once more born to them, they call the child *Natha—i.e.*, one having a *Nath* or nose ring. They pierce the child's nose, and introduce a nose ring (an ornament worn by girls and women only), with the desire that the little one should be mistaken for a girl, and so passed over by the evil spirits. Also, if an elder brother has died, a boy is clothed very shabbily, no doubt because it is hoped that he will thus escape the notice of the godlings—the agents of divine mischief in India. This idea is not unknown in Europe. Some years ago, when spending a summer in the Engadine, we there met an Italian lady, a Milanese. She was accompanied by a sweet little child about five or six years of age. For some days the little one went about attired in a knicker-bocker suit, and of course was thought to be a boy, until one day to our amazement it appeared dressed as a girl in a pretty white muslin frock. On astonishment being expressed at the transformation, the child's mother said that out of a large family which she had had, the only survivors were one grown-up son and this little girl ; those she had lost between were all girls ; she seemed to think that by disguising the sex of this one she would in some way divert evil from it.

In India a not uncommon method of disposing of an enemy is to mix small bits of chopped hair with his food. This is said to have a most deadly effect, unless an emetic be speedily given.

The so-called devil-dancers or diviners of Ceylon fabricate a singular kind of charm, which is supposed to have the effect of killing an enemy, consisting of a tiny wooden figure of a man, about eight inches in length. The body of the image is stuck all over with pins, placed in a small clay coffin, and then buried. As it decays, so will the person whom it represents pine away and die.

This, it seems scarcely necessary to state, recalls a custom known to have been in use in Europe in the Middle Ages, when waxen figures were made of an enemy, stuck full of pins, and then exposed to the sun or a fire until the wax melted. Neapolitans—if they have a spite against any one—administer chopped hair to his dog or his cat. The customs of the East and the West are mixed up in these cases in a manner that is, to say the least, very remarkable.

At Mayence on the Rhine, a singular superstition prevails, even amongst the upper classes. They believe that should any one be buried in one of their former garments which has their name in full marked upon it, seven members of that family will die within a brief space of time afterwards. My informant heard this from a near relation of hers, a young lady, who fully believed it, and at the time of her father's death was much distressed to find that he had been thus interred. The first-named lady added that, curious to relate, in this case the prophecy had come true, several near relations of the younger lady (she was not quite sure whether it was *seven* exactly) had died very shortly after the decease of her father.

NOTE. —*Evil-eye* (Greek *phthonos*) : how it operated on the sufferer is explained by Heliodorus (*Æthiopica*, iii. 8) as a sort of infection communicated chiefly through the eyes. *Conf.* King's *Gnostics*, p. 113.

CHAPTER XI

THE WILD HUNTSMAN OF NORTHERN EUROPE AND HIS POSSIBLE ASIATIC ORIGIN

GENERAL SIR ALEXANDER CUNNINGHAM, in the Preface to his *Bhilsa Topes*, 1854 (page 7), expressed an opinion that the Welsh word Buddwâs, and the Saxon name *Woden*, are " but slightly altered forms of the word Buddha. The fourth day of the week, Wednesday, or *Woden's-day*, was named *Dies Mercurii* by the Romans, and is still called Budhwâr by the Hindûs. Maia was the mother of the Greek Hermeias, or Hermes, and Mâyâ was the mother of the Indian Buddha. The connection between Hermes, Buddwâs, Woden, and Buddha is evident, although it may be difficult, and perhaps nearly impossible, to make it apparent to the general reader." [1]

About twenty-seven years ago, M. Holmböe, in his work entitled *Buddhisme en Norvège*, endeavoured to prove that the Scandinavian god Odin, if not Buddha himself, was one of his disciples. M. Holmböe was of opinion that the missions of the Buddhists did not stop in Transoxiana and Upper Asia,

[1] This is all based on a false etymology. *Budha*, and not *Buddha*, is the Sanskrit for Mercury or Hermes. The meaning of Budha is wise, prudent, and that of Buddha is perfectly enlightened. Budhwar, and not Buddhwâr, is Wednesday, or Mercury's day, to the Hindûs ; and it means Mercury's, and never Buddha's, day to them. If there be anything to connect Wednesday and Budhwâr etymologically, such derivation would connect Woden with Budha (Mercury) and *not* with Buddha. This, and other portions of *Bhilsa Topes*, would probably be extensively recast if another edition were to be brought out.

but that they pushed on still further, through Persia, towards the Caucasus, and from thence to the homes of the ancestors of the present Scandinavians, when they were still in the countries east and north of the Russia of the present day. Relations being established with them, it is easy to conceive that they were continued, and that Buddhist doctors of religion afterwards visited Scandinavia ; and it is also not impossible that the most illustrious of these missionaries were called, if not " Buddha," at least by some epithet derived from the same Sanscrit root *budh*, " to know, to understand " : as for example, *bôdhin*, "making known, teaching, revealing"; or *bôdhat*, *bôdhant*, the present participle of the verb ; and that from this appellation the Scandinavians may have formed *Odin*, and the Germans *Woden*. The hypothesis, which thus seeks to identify Odin with Buddha, or with some of the missionaries of the Buddhist faith, would be at least a plausible one, if only in Hindûstan the name for Wednesday or Woden's-day had in any way the meaning of Buddha's day. In Scandinavia it is *Onsdag*, a contraction for Odin's-day.

As an aid towards giving Odin the Asiatic origin which is thus claimed for him, it might be observed that his special symbol was the *triskele* or three-armed sun-snake, figured on Plate I, fig. 12. As we have already seen, the *Svastika*, the emblem of fire and lightning, was the symbol of Thor.

It is true that in those northern lands Odin is represented as a warrior, but the sword has often accompanied religion. It seems hardly necessary to remind our readers that the Christian Church owes much of its progress to the sword. Germany produced not a few warlike proselytisers :

none more celebrated than St Ulrich, Bishop of Augsburg in the tenth century (923-973), and his contemporaries or immediate successors, Gerhard, Gebehard, and Berns.

Odin may have been successful in his religious crusade, and have taken a place at first amongst the inferior gods. Adam of Bremen, as quoted by Grimm, *Deutche Mythologie*, is of opinion that this was the case, because in the temple at Old Upsala in Sweden, the statue of Thor occupied the place of honour between Odin and Frey the Sun-god— adding that after a time Odin came to be ranked amongst the superior gods. In his capacity of superior god Odin was the storm god, according to Kelly, in his *Indo-European Traditions and Folk-Lore*. The name *Woden* or *Wuotan* denotes the strong and furious goer : Gothic, *Wods* ; Norwegian, *o'dr*, enraged. According to this view, the name may therefore be closely allied to the Lowland Scotch word *wud*, mad or furious. A Jacobite song of 1745 says, "the women are a' gane *wud*." There is also a Scotch proverb, "Dinna put a knife into a *wud* man's hand." Odin, as the storm god, may well be supposed to have ridden like one *wud* : he has been considered to be the Wild Huntsman of the German legends. If so, the legend of the Erl King or Wild Huntsman probably came from the same source as Odin's Wild Hunt. He, and his wife Freyja, are fabled to have had two sons, Baldr and Hermond. The tale runs thus : Freyja had made all created things swear that they would never hurt Baldr, "that whitest and most beloved of the gods ;" however there was one little shoot "that groweth East of Valhalla, so small and delicate that she forgot to take its oath." It was the mistletoe, and with a branch of that feeble plant, flung by the hand of the blind Hodr, Baldr was struck dead. He then descended into the gloomy snake-covered Helheim, whither Hermond (Baldr's brother) made a violent but unsuccessful ride from star-spangled Valhalla, mounted on Sleipner, his father's horse, in order to obtain his brother's body. The Hel Jagd, as it is called in some parts of Germany, has by others been styled the English Hunt. Both refer to the nether world; we have already seen (*ante* Chap VII) that Great Britain was formerly supposed to be the Land of Departed Souls.

The late Kamer Herr Dr Worsaae was of opinion that the inferior gods were always represented clothed, and those of a superior order naked, with a girdle only, or *sky clad* as the Jains of India term it. If this be the invariable rule, it seems not impossible that the man on horseback in the brooch in my possession, figured on Plate XVIII, fig. 1, may have been intended for Odin himself after he had been exalted to the highest grade in the Scandinavian Pantheon.

The above quoted authority was of opinion that the worship of Odin in Scandinavia dates from what is styled the *Earlier Iron Age* in those countries—which occupied the first 450 years A.D.; and he held that it extended down to the so-called *Middle Iron Age, i.e.,* 700 A.D. In the example given, the man is unquestionably *sky clad*, and the dog may pass for a greyhound, which was Odin's dog. In the German, as well as in the Aryan mythology, the dog is an embodiment of the wind and also an attendant upon the dead. The German name for a greyhound is *Wind-hund*.

We would here draw attention to fig. 2 on this Plate,

a specimen of the same type of brooch as fig. 1 ; its subject is different, but it seems to belong to the same period. No. 2, was found in an ancient grave near Bregenz on the Lake of Constance, together with another brooch also of a Norwegian character : these two latter, probably also date from the earlier Iron Age of Scandinavia. The only way in which we can reasonably account for the presence of such objects, so far away from their original home, is—that when the Swedes took Bregenz by stratagem, about two hundred years ago, Norwegian soldiers formed a part of their army, and that some of these were buried with their ornaments as they fell, and again that these two brooches must either have been reproductions of the old forms, or have been preserved for generations as heirlooms.

To return to Odin, Dr Hans Hildebrand, in his *Manual of Scandinavian Art*, gives an illustration of a warrior on horseback on an embossed bronze which was found at Vendel in Sweden. This figure is armed with a circular shield and a heavy spear, it is preceded and followed by a bird, and a serpent is in the act of raising itself to sting one of the horse's fore-legs. Dr Hildebrand is of opinion that this is doubtless a mythological subject, and presumes that its correct explanation is to be found not very far off. He says, " The horseman is *Wodan* who, according to the Scandinavian legends, had a heavy spear, and was, as here represented, attended by two ravens, which brought him news from all over the world." He adds—" The serpent attacking the horse, reminds us of the mythological *Midgards* serpent, or the serpent encircling the central world, the implacable enemy of the gods."

When in India in 1891-92, we were much interested in various incidents related to us by a Russian gentleman, Prince Galitzin, touching his travels through Central Asia. At that time he had been in India a year—possibly more. He had come thither from his own country *via* Samarkand, Yarkand, and over the Karakoram to Leh and Kashmir; he purposed on his return journey to take the same or a somewhat similar route. He told us a curious fact which seems to demonstrate the foundation of the tradition which ascribes to Odin an Asiatic origin, and to serve also to bear out Dr Hildebrand's conjectures regarding the bronze relic above described. Prince Galitzin stated that one or more ravens frequently join and accompany caravans part of the way on that journey, attaching themselves to them at a particular point on the route —viz., that at which they have to pass over bare plains or steppes, these birds keep for days together with a caravan. Such an occurrence as ravens following parties of people is, we believe, unknown in Europe. As regards Odin, in his character of the Wild Huntsman, the following is worthy of consideration :—

On landing at Christiania in the summer of 1883, we remarked the extraordinary resemblance borne by the horses in the ordinary street carriages of that city to a certain breed in Central Asia, called *Yarkandis*, from their home in Yarkand : we are well acquainted with the type, having possessed and ridden many of them in the northern portion of the Himâlayas, and are therefore not likely to have been mistaken in the likeness. The Norwegian horses have the same general form, the same head and neck, the same dark line down the spine, and the zebra-like markings on the legs peculiar to the

Yarkandis, facts which seem to prove that they, like the Yarkandis, are of an unmixed race, and still retain their aboriginal characteristics.   When remarking to a Norwegian gentleman on the wonderful similarity of the horses of his country to those of Central Asia, he said, " The people in my part of Norway say that Odin brought horses from the Himâlayas." The director of the Museum at Bergen, when told of the striking likeness between the animals, observed, " that it was well known from certain records that the horse was introduced into Norway about 2000 years ago, or about the time when Odin is fabled to have first arrived on the scene ; but he did not credit the tradition that this hero brought them, or even that he ever existed."   As regards the introduction of the horse into Scandinavia, Dr Blombery, the then assistant-director of the Historical Museum at Stockholm, was of opinion that the horse was known in Sweden during the later Stone Age ; but when this period began, or when it ended, or when the Bronze Age, which succeeded it, commenced, no one has yet been able to determine, though some seem to think it probable that the Iron Age in Scandinavia dates from shortly before the Christian era.   But, as regards those northern lands, we must not fail to keep in mind that their inhabitants were pagans down to the eleventh century, and we may therefore, perhaps, put the commencement of the Iron Age at a later period than that given above.

CHAPTER XII

ARCHITECTURAL AND OTHER CUSTOMS

IN all, or nearly all, the houses in the more elevated Himâlayan villages, the cow stall forms the ground floor of the
house ; the same style of building prevails also amongst those
who inhabit high or mountainous districts in Europe. All the
peasants' houses in the Engadine, and in some other parts of
Switzerland, are built in this fashion, partly for the purpose of
raising the living and sleeping rooms above ground level, and
also because during their severe winters the ascending breath
of the animals gives some additional warmth to the rooms
above. The inconvenience of passing through the cow stall
to the family apartments is obviated in the Engadine by a
flight of steps on either side of the door of approach to the
first floor : the place of entrance for the cattle is in the centre
of the basement. In some parts of the North of Spain also
the houses are built on the same plan, but there it is necessary
to steer one's way through the cows, goats, and pigs which
inhabit the ground floor, in order to arrive at the staircase
leading to the upper rooms. The first floor rooms in Spain
are usually devoted to the storage of grain, roots, etc. ; on
the floor above this again are the sitting and bed rooms,
which, contrary perhaps to what we might expect, are spotlessly clean. Another type of house is found equally in
exposed situations in the Northern Himâlayas, in many

178

parts of Switzerland and in Norway, the roof being composed of rough boards kept in position by large stones.

The Norwegian peasant's storehouse, figured on Plate
XXI, might stand for an almost exact reproduction of certain
superior native houses existing twenty years ago in Śrînagar,
the capital of Kashmir,[1] and of those of the Lahaul valley in
the Himâlayas.   The drawing in question is taken from one
of the very best specimens of such store-houses still remaining
in Norway.   The windows, or rather the shutters, for there is
no glass in them, open precisely like those of Kashmir houses.
The general construction is the same also : the resemblance
extended formerly even to the man and horse sculptured
on the front gable ; the rest of the ornamentation likewise,
was almost identical in character.   It would appear that both
in Norway and in the Himâlayas, in order to form the walls
of such structures, large logs of wood were placed horizontally
one above the other, in the form of a square, and dovetailed
together at the four corners, no nails being employed ; the
interstices between the logs being filled in with dry moss.
The roofs of the better class of houses in Kashmir and also
in Norway—as will be seen from the drawing—consist merely
of planks of wood ;   but the smaller and poorer houses,
especially those in mountainous districts in Asia which
are in tolerably sheltered situations, and those in some
parts of Norway, are not so carefully finished as the one
on this Plate.   A roofing of earth and grass sods, over the
rafters, is substituted for the planking—an advantage from

[1] In the interval, the city has experienced several most destructive fires ; houses
have been rebuilt on more economical and less picturesque lines : none of this lovely
old type seems to be left now.

an artistic point of view—for in summer the roof becomes a luxuriant bed of wild flowers : not unfrequently several small trees also take root there. So much for secular architecture : let us now turn our attention awhile to sacred buildings.

A common feature in the Muhammedan Mosques of India, is a propylon or lofty arched gateway flanked on either side by a graceful and slender minaret ; a propylon sometimes forms the entrance gateway to the courtyard of a mosque ; but most frequently it is placed against the chief entrance of the Mosque itself, towers above it, and, unless the structure be viewed from some distance, conceals its several domes. One would not perhaps be surprised to find buildings in the South of France which recall Moorish Art, but he is certainly not a little astonished to discover traces of a purely Muhammedan architectural feature in Europe. Two or three years ago, when travelling by rail from Pau to Toulouse, we passed by several small villages which were quite close to the line. Most, if not all the churches in that district have, or have had, such a frontage ; in some, the propylon seemed to be detached from the church, but formed the approach to it ; in others, again, the church had apparently disappeared, or what was possibly more likely to be the case —owing to its being detached—was hidden from view by other buildings ; but the propylon or pyramid-like gateway is there, standing majestically with its minarets on either side of it.

A marked type of religious architecture exists amongst various Hindû or Hindûized peoples all over the Himâlayas —in Nêpâl, in Kulu, and in Kashmir. Their temples are wooden structures : they are for the most part placed in forests or in groves of the sacred deodâra.

The Nêpâli temple at Benares figured on Plate XX will be sufficient to show the general form and construction of such buildings. This temple overlooks the Ganges : it was erected by a Mahârâjâ of Nêpâl about 200 years ago. It is a large square wooden building, elevated on a platform about four feet in height. The principal entrance is approached by a short flight of steps ; on either side of this is a lion carved in stone. On the right hand, between the steps and the lion, is a stone bust of Śiva in alto-rilievo. The hair is arranged in a double row of curls below the ears, the curls stand out like the rays of the sun, and round the neck of the statue are coiled most life-like snakes. The temple has four doors : each door has a window on either side of it. These doors, as well as the shutters of the windows, are richly carved, and over each is a segment of a pointed arch, surmounted by the well-known chhatrî or umbrella of royalty. Sloping eaves, about six feet wide, roofed with small tiles and supported on wooden brackets, project all round the lower story ; above this is a square second story of smaller dimensions furnished with similar sloping eaves : all along their outer edge are hung small bells at short distances from each other, so as to tinkle at the slightest breath of wind. Above this again, is a kind of kiosk, with a high pinnacled roof; smaller kiosks of the same form occupy the four corners of its platform. From an iron rod on the summit a large bell is suspended; and a *trisul* or trident, one of the emblems of Śiva, is also attached to the central kiosk : the roofs of the kiosks and the trident also are gilt. Close to this temple is a dharmaśâlâ, or house of rest for pilgrims, erected by the Mahârâjâ who built the temple. In the Hindû temples of the Western Himâlayas there are many other specimens of the same style of architecture, one such exists a short distance below Nachar in the Satlaj valley, another at Manâlî in the Kulu valley—both in groves of the deodâra, the sacred tree of those parts. We see it again universally repeated in the wooden Mosques of Kashmir, which of course are Muhammedan structures. Being personally acquainted with these examples, we can affirm that the type in each is precisely similar. It is singular to find the same form reproduced in the oldest church architecture of Norway, as will be seen on referring to Plate XIX, on which is represented the ancient church of Borgund in the Laerdal, built in the eleventh century, *i.e.*, soon after the introduction of Christianity into Scandinavia. By many it has been likened to a Chinese Pagoda.

If we admit that the remote ancestors of the builders of this church came from Asia, it becomes easy to imagine that in its construction they adopted Eastern forms which had been preserved amongst them by long tradition : for how can we otherwise account for the circumstance that, though living in a high northern latitude, where daylight in winter is very brief, their chief object would seem to have been to exclude both Sun and light, and conceal the windows by making a deep verandah and sloping eaves round the exterior of the building, after the fashion of native and European builders in India ? In the case of the Borgund Church, slabs of stone having a uniform height of about eight inches, were placed on the ground at intervals ; the wooden uprights and cross pieces rest on these, to which the structure owes its preservation. Starting from the base of the exterior, a row of sloping eaves forms the roof of a verandah which encircles the basement; a second row of eaves protects the walls of the lower half of the Church; a third forms the roof of the nave; a fifth and sixth row would seem to have been added for the sake of giving symmetry to the whole. The quaint objects on the third and fourth roofs are dragons' heads with projecting tongues, an ornament which forcibly recalls that on Oriental and Chinese buildings. This most interesting monument is well worth studying. It has been purchased by an Archæological Society, who have restored it and intend to keep it in repair. The key is kept at a neighbouring small farm house.

We will here quote from an Italian translation of the work of Tavernier, a famous French traveller (published at Bologna in 1690 and entitled *Viaggie nella Turchia, Persia, e Indiè*) the following description of a temple at Benares which existed in his day, but was afterwards destroyed by the orders of the Moghul Emperor Aurangzeb. It runs as follows: "The Pagoda at Banaras is the most famous in all India, after that of Jagannath. They may be called almost equal, and both are situated near the banks of the river Ganges in the respective cities whence they derive their names." This of course is not correct, for the Jagannâth temple is situated at Pûrî in Orissa. "From the door of the Pagoda at Banaras, one descends by steps down to the river, on these steps are at intervals small platforms with very dark little rooms, in some of which the Brahmans live; others they use as kitchens, in which to prepare their food, because these idolaters, after having washed themselves, said their prayers, and made their offerings in the Pagoda, prepare their food themselves, fearing lest another, not in a condition of ceremonial purity, should touch it. But above all they drink with much devotion of the water of the Ganges, imagining that by so doing they will be freed from all stain of sin. To return to the Pagoda, which is built *in the form of a cross, as are all the other temples.* In the centre of the exterior rises an immensely high cupola, constructed somewhat like a high tower, which has many sides to it, and terminates in a point. At each of the four ends of the cross is a small tower, which one can ascend from the exterior. Before reaching the top, there are several balconies and niches, which give exit into the open air, and around are sculptured figures consisting of every kind of mis-shapen animal. In the interior of the building, immediately beneath the large cupola, is an altar seven or eight feet long, and six feet in width, which has two small flights of steps serving as *predellas* (seats for the priests) and covered with a beautiful carpet, which is sometimes of gold stuff, and sometimes of silk, according to the solemnity of the day or festival.

"The altars (of the Hindûs generally) are covered with gold or silver brocade, or with some lovely painted material. The altar in this Pagoda is so arranged that it, and the idols which are upon it, can be seen from without the entrance door ; because neither women nor young girls are permitted to enter nor (even) the men of one of their tribes (castes ?), but have to pay their devotions outside. Amongst the idols which stand on the altar there is one which is five or six feet high ; its body, arms, and legs are not visible, but only the head and neck, all the rest being covered with a robe which trails down to the ground. Sometimes this idol wears a rich gold chain round its throat, or an ornament of rubies or pearls, or emeralds. The idol was made in remembrance and in the likeness of Bain-madu " (Vishnu or Mâdhava) " whom they consider to have been a very great personage,— a saint, whose name they are constantly invoking. On the left hand of the altar is a figure of an animal, or rather of some mythological creature, partly elephant, partly horse, partly mule. It is of massive gold, and is called by them Guru " (Garuda ?) " which no one but a Brahman is ever allowed to approach. Near the entrance to the Pagoda, between the great door and the high altar (above described), one sees a smaller altar on the left hand, upon which is an idol in black marble, seated with its legs crossed and about two feet in height. When I entered, a boy was standing on the left hand of it, the son of the chief priest, who kept touching the idol with pieces of silk and embroidered cloths of the shape of handkerchiefs, which he afterwards returned to those who gave them to him for this purpose. Some of the people also gave this lad chains made of beads, which looked like the stones of some fruit and had a very sweet odour, others, what looked like rosaries made of coral and amber ; and some chains of flowers. The idolaters wear these chains round their necks, or say their prayers over these beads. The idol on the small altar is called Morli Ram " (Muralidhar, *i.e.*, Krishna) " that is the god Morli who they say is the brother of the one on the high altar." [1]

[1] The translation of Morli Ram by the god Morli is very interesting, as showing that in Tavernier's time, as at the present day, the name Râma was employed frequently by Hindus to mean "god" irrespective of the particular "god" meant.

In the above description, the ground plan of the temple, which has the form of a cross as have all the other Pagodas, and the *image* of which only the head is visible, the rest of the body being enveloped in a rich robe, also the *presentation of flowers, strings of beads*, or other objects, to the image that they may be sanctified by contact with it—recall much that is familiar to us in modern European Christianity. The same traveller speaks too of another fine building near this Pagoda, a College built by the then Râjâ, in which some of his own sons, and other lads of good caste were receiving education at the hands of the resident Brâhmans. On the left hand, at the entrance to the college, the Râjâ had erected a Pagoda, which was closed at the time of Tavernier's visit; but as he much wished to see the interior, he made enquiries, and was told that in order to do so he must present himself at the door before sunrise on the following morning, which he accordingly did. On his arrival there, he found an immense concourse of men, women, and children awaiting the opening of the door. He shall give his own account of what he witnessed on that occasion. "At the hour fixed, eight Brahmans advanced, four on each side of the door of the Pagoda, each having a thurible in his hands. There were also many other Brahmans who made a great noise with drums and other instruments. The two oldest amongst them sang one of their own hymns, the people joining in, all having in their hands a peacock's tail, or some other kind of fan to chase away the flies, so that when the door of the Pagoda was opened the idol might not be incommoded by them. This driving away of the flies with music lasted half an hour, or until the two chief Brahmans made a very great noise with bells at three distinct intervals ; after which they tapped the door with a mallet. On this being done, the door was immediately opened by six Brahmans, who were within the Pagoda. In the interior, about six or eight paces distant from the entrance was an altar on which was a female idol, called by them Ram Ram[1] who was the sister of Morli Ram. She had on her right hand a boy like a Cupid, called the god Lakemin " (Lakshmana), "and on her left arm she carried an image of a female child, called the goddess Sita.[2]

" The door of the temple being opened, and the curtain drawn back, the people, as soon as they saw the idol, all prostrated themselves three times with their faces to the ground, putting their hands above their heads, and when they stood up again they presented (as in the other Pagoda) bunches of flowers and strings of beads, in order that they might be made to touch the idol. In front of the altar stood an old Brahman who held in his hands a lamp with nine lighted wicks, on which he from time to time dropped a species of incense, putting the lamp close to the idol."

This last point leads us to remark on the common use of incense in religious worship in India, amongst both Hindûs and Jains. When staying on Mount Abû in Râjpûtânâ we saw at least fifty Jaina pilgrims, men, women and children perform a part of their devotions, after they had made their

---

[1] This must be meant for Râmachandra a male and not a female deity, and mythologically a relative (bhâi also " brother") of Muralîdhar or Krishna : perhaps his invariable representation as a young hairless boy misled Tavernier.

[2] This settles the identity of Ram Ram with Râmachandra, as male deities are usually represented as having their wives on a much smaller scale than themselves, seated on their thighs.

offerings in the innermost shrine of one of the Jaina temples
—whither, of course, we could not follow them.   This done,
they all seated themselves in the *Mantapa* or porch of the
temple in a large circle, and were then censed by the
attendant priest.

The form of the censer and its chains was precisely such
as may be seen in any Roman Catholic Church.   Incense
is said to have been offered by the ancient Egyptians.
Plutarch says, that resin was offered in the morning to
purify and remove the bad odours of the night and early
morn, myrrh at noon, and about sunset an aromatic compound called *kuphi*.   Incense would appear to have been
unknown in the Christian Church in connection with the
Holy Eucharist until the time of St Gregory the Great,
or the latter part of the 6th century A.D.   After this
period, its use became general in churches.   Some Romish
writers have tried to trace its use up to the Apostolic age,
although no mention of it occurs in the writings of the
first three centuries of our era, with the exception of the
Apostolic Canons which speak of incense at the time of
oblation : these Canons, however, cannot, it is said, be proved
to have existed before the 3rd century.   The first reference
to them as an entire collection was made in 325 A.D. by the
Council of Nice.   The Qâlmak (Calmuck) Tartars, who
are Buddhists, also use incense in their worship.   Their
chief priest is styled the *Kutuchta*, and in former days was
subject to the Dalai Lama of Tibet ; but in course of time
schisms arose, and he established himself on an equal foot-
ing with his superior.   The *Kutuchta* never exposes himself
to public gaze except on certain particular days, when with

much pomp and ceremony he is carried in procession to a tent covered with velvet, where he sits cross-legged on a throne, with the Lâmas on cushions around him, and a figure on each side representing the divine essence. The whole assembly then prostrate themselves on the ground, and burst out into loud acclamations in praise of the Deity and lofty eulogiums upon the *Kutuchta*. The Lâmas next throw odoriferous herbs into their censers, with which they perfume the figures, the pontiff and the whole congregation.

Cow-dung, as we all know, is a " sacred " object in India ; and in very ancient days, at least, it seems to have been so in Europe, for Winckelmann, who wrote in the last century, mentions in his *History of Ancient Art* that Pamphôs, one of the most ancient Greek poets, describes a statue of Zeus as being covered with cow-dung. The German savant imagined this to indicate that the presence of the divinity extends to all objects, even the most abject. No such error could be committed now, since India is so much better known than it was in his day, and all who have been in that country are aware that cow-dung is commonly employed by the natives as a sacred purifier. Such a purification, for instance, would be necessary, should a man, who possesses " caste," drink out of a cup or glass which had been used by Europeans, or by one not of his own caste.

Passing from sacred to familiar personal customs, we would draw attention to that of the "cradle board" system of carrying children about. From discoveries made at various times in the graves, barrows, and cists of different prehistoric peoples, it has been gathered that the practice of carrying a young child about on a flat "cradle board" prevailed in Britain and the North of Europe, and it is considered very probable that the same custom was in use at one time over a great part of the world. It would seem that the modern custom in Bavaria and in other parts of Germany, both amongst the higher and lower classes, of dressing their infants very lightly—usually one cotton garment only—and placing it on its back on a large pillow folded over the body, leaving the head alone visible, is a survival of the ancient cradle board.

In the matter of shoes, too, there is much similarity sometimes between the East and the more uncivilized parts of the West. Sir A. Mitchell, in his most interesting work, *The Past in the Present*, says: " I once met a funeral procession in the Highlands of Scotland, in which one of the men who carried the coffin wore shoes made of the untanned hide of the ox, with the hair still on it. Such shoes are known as *rivilins*, and are described in books of costumes as the shoes of the ancient Britons. They are correctly so described, and have properly a place in collections of antiquities; and yet it happens that there are thousands of people in Scotland who wear this shoe at this hour. It is in most common use in Shetland, where thousands of pairs could at this moment be purchased, and likewise in the Hebrides. There is probably no older form of shoe known. It is nothing but a piece of untanned hide folded when fresh, or moistened and placed up the sides of the foot and over the toes, and then stitched or closed at the heel and toes with a piece of twine or a thong of hide, and then secured to the foot, more or less like a sandal."

A similar species of foot covering can also be now seen on the borders of Central Asia, where shoes on the model of the *rivilins* above described are worn by the Ladâkhis of both sexes. The climate of Ladâkh being a more inclement one than that of the Scottish Isles, the Ladâkhis make for themselves leggings of pattû, a fabric made of the undyed wool of the white sheep. They then take a piece of raw hide, let it dry to the shape of the foot, cut it to the required size, and stitch it firmly round the foot and on to the legging. In very cold weather, when about to take a journey, they put as much flour as they can inside this foot covering, with the double purpose of keeping their feet warm and of having with them an additional supply of food in case of need. In certain districts in Italy a shoe of the same kind is still worn by the people. It is not an uncommon sight for peasants to be walking about Rome and in the Campagna with foot coverings of the same nature as those of the Scottish Isles and of Western Tibet—all being equally rude in form, evidently made on the foot, and fastened with twine or thongs of hide.

As a very curious instance of the development of European and Asiatic ideas in the same direction, and also to illustrate the old adage that " there is nothing new under the sun," we mention here the fact that the ordinary telephone (not the electric one, of course) has been known to and used by the natives of India for many generations. A friend (since retired from the Indian public service) had, when we were staying with him in Dehli, a native servant as bearer or valet, who had been many years in his employ. When any new or interesting discovery was made in Europe, his master was in the habit of telling him about it. On the ordinary telephone being first spoken of, this gentleman mentioned it to his native servant, enlarging upon what might eventually be its use, when to his amazement the man replied: " Oh, Sahib, we natives have known of such things for a long time. My father and my grandfather used one I know ; and every day I talk with a fellow servant across the Sahib's compound in that manner!" On being requested to produce his instrument, the servant went out and speedily returned with two pieces of bamboo each about eight inches in length, and an inch or an inch and a half in diameter. One end of each tube was covered with a bit of parchment, through which a string from 60 to 100 feet long was passed, and thus connected them. It perfectly answered the purpose of communication from one side of the compound to the other. The same method is said also to be adopted by the natives of some parts of the Himâlayas, who talk thus to each other across deep ravines.

CHAPTER XIII

SPAIN, OR FURTHER EUROPE

THE extraordinary dissimilarity between many of the manners and customs of Spain and those of other nations in Europe, renders the title "further Europe" not inappropriate, if used in the sense that Burma and Siam are "further India." Many differences are no doubt due to the occupation of portions of the Spanish Peninsula by the Moors, which lasted for some centuries. A survival of Moorish ways is to be seen in the dress of Spanish women of all classes, the mantilla resembles the *fonta*, the head covering of modern Moorish women in Algeria. Again, Spanish churches have very rarely, if ever, any seats or benches in them. The men either stand or kneel during the services, the women of the people, when not kneeling, sit upon their heels, or not unfrequently seat themselves cross-legged upon the pavement. Women of the upper classes, and invalids, take their own camp-stools with them when they go to church. As in Muhammedan mosques, where certain portions are covered with matting, so in Spanish churches a considerable space in front of the high altar is covered in this manner.

The city of Toledo (its Archbishop is the Primate of all Spain) is generally believed to have had a considerable Christian population at the time it was conquered by the Moors, when a good many of the Christians either fled or were killed in battle. Some, however, remained, bowed themselves to the yoke of the conqueror, and were unmolested in the exercise of their religion. A reminiscence of this circumstance is preserved in the well-known curious fact that in a chapel within the walls of the Cathedral at Toledo, what is called the Mus-Arabic[1] ritual is still followed. It differs so much from the present Roman Catholic rite, which goes on in the same building, and frequently at the same hour, that the priests and all who serve in the Mus-Arabic chapel have to receive a special training. On Easter Monday, 1884, when we assisted at the 8 o'clock mass in this chapel, barely more than thirty worshippers were present, possibly because the Archbishop was then celebrating high mass at the high altar. The service was not an ornate one, and in some particulars was not unlike our Anglican ritual; a few peculiarities are worthy of notice. On the credence table was a crucifix about ten inches high, also a pair of tall, lighted candles, some high candles were also as usual on the altar; but just before the celebrant began the office, the serving priest or deacon placed a small lighted taper on it. On his way from the choir to the altar, the officiating priest intoned certain Latin sentences; whilst ascending the steps he repeated the words: "I will wash my hands in innocency, O Lord, and so will I go to Thine altar,"—a vessel of water being presented to him, in which he dipped his hands. Another remarkable incident in the service was,

---

[1] "Mos-Arabic, or Mus-Arabic, Mos-Arabian, etc., are all corruptions of *Mut-'arrib*, an Arab half-breed, an impure Arab, or one who would pass for an Arab." Therefore the Mus-Arabic ritual would apparently mean that of the Arab or Moorish half-breeds of Spain.

that at the moment of the Consecration of the Host, instead of the ordinary little bell to inform the worshippers that the supreme act is taking place, a curious machine fixed near a window, and facing the altar, was put in motion by one of the canons or inferior clergy present, who pulled a rope, and then allowed the apparatus to return upon itself.[1]

It was formed of flat pieces of wood so arranged that they looked like the spokes of a water-wheel, working apparently on a common pivot.   As the wheel revolved, each spoke dropped down on the one beneath it, this caused a sound resembling a loud clapper or an old-fashioned watchman's rattle.   Similar clappers, but of course on a much larger scale, are fixed on the top of the towers of churches in Spain.   They are used during the latter part of Holy Week, both to announce the hours of worship and the time of day, since bells are not then allowed to be rung, and all clocks are stopped.[2]   The popular opinion is, that the bells of Spain make a journey to Rome during those three days, nor are they singular in this, for the bells of the village of Orly (Dept. Seine, France) are believed by its inhabitants to do the same.   They appear, however, to have no substitute for them, but on the Thursday, Friday, and Saturday in Holy Week, the choir boys of that place, as stated by M. Fouju in the *Revue des*

---

[1] Possibly, at the time of the foundation of this chapel, bells were unknown in Spain.

[2] This custom exists also in Naples, but there, though the church bells and the clocks are mute, no clapper is substituted for the bells, except in private houses, where a kind of watchman's rattle is used to give notice of the meals, instead of the usual dinner-bell.

Traditions Populaires, May 1890, sometimes go about with a curious little wooden instrument of very rude construction in their hands. It consists of a flat piece of wood, in form somewhat like an hour-glass, it is from seven to eight inches in length, by about three inches in width ; through the centre of it is passed another piece of wood, one end of this serves as a handle, the other extremity projects about two inches only ; to this is attached a moveable tiny mallet, which, when the instrument is shaken in the proper direction, strikes alternately on the upper and lower ends of the body of the instrument, and gives out a sound very similar to the little machine commonly used in Paris by the peripatetic vendors of *gauffres* and *plaisirs*, the delight of French children. The name of this curious little instrument is *Toque Maillot* (literally hit mallet). It would appear that this custom is not observed every year, but only if amongst the choristers of any particular year some of them are big boys. On such occasions, they go from house to house with their *Toque Maillot*, taking with them some Holy Water, and singing :—

> "Alleluia with all our heart,
> We are children of the choir,
> The day will come, when GOD takes you, Alleluia."

They thus collect a good deal of money, every one gives them sous or eggs. At Easter, the *Toque Maillot* is put away, and does not reappear until the same time some other year.

In the Island of Corfu also the bells are mute, and the clocks are stopped the last days of Holy Week, but at 11 A.M. on the Saturday morning the whole town seems to have gone mad. All of a sudden a most fearful noise and Babel of sounds ensues, bells ring their loudest, guns are fired off in all directions, and crockery is thrown out of the windows. A few minutes before that hour men may be seen standing at the doors of various houses holding a lamb with one hand and a knife in the other. They are awaiting the signal to kill the animal for their Easter dinner. The firing continues the whole of the day; it has a most curious effect upon all the dogs of the place, they tear out of the town as though seized with hydrophobia, and do not return until all is quiet again. With regard to throwing crockery down into the street, such a quantity is disposed of in this manner that the pot-sherds of the past year must have been accumulated for this purpose. She is a happy woman who can contrive to hit a Jew with one of her fragments. Experience would seem, however, to have taught that race that discretion is the better part of valour: the Jews are said rarely to leave their houses on that day. Both those who fire off guns, and the smashers of old crockery, give as their reason for doing so that their intention is to kill the arch-traitor, Judas Iscariot! Mons. Hippolite Pirou, in his *Voyage a l'île de Cuba*, Paris, 1876, states that the Jews are most intensely detested there. On the Saturday in Holy Week, at the time the Hallelujah is sung, the bells are made to ring in a most singular manner, they give out the strangest sounds it is possible to imagine, added to which the firing off of guns all over the town, renders the whole almost unbearable. The youths of the place and all the little street boys are in a high state of delight and excitement; it is they who are the prime movers and organisers of the whole affair.

With the object of burning the Jews in effigy, some days

beforehand they prepare life-sized dummy figures, they cari-
cature both sexes, dressing up these figures in ridiculous costumes, giving the male ones enormous false collars and
exaggerated attire, and putting the shabbiest old dresses on
the female ones. On the Saturday morning these figures are
hung up in the middle of the streets, the young men and
lads armed with fowling-pieces and pistols, await the signal
with impatience, and as soon as the bells begin to sound, with
gestures of rage and abhorrence, they shoot at these *Judios*,
as they call them, at the same time igniting the fireworks
attached to these figures, and also striking them and spitting
in their faces. This is carried on until nothing remains of
them but a heap of ashes.

According to the Cubans, all Jews ought to be burnt
alive. "Did not these *perros di Judios* (dogs of Jews) put
Christ to death?" say they. If a Spaniard wishes to insult
any one he calls him a Jew.

It seems highly probable that the clapper was the primitive Christian mode of calling the people to worship before
bells were invented. In evidence of this, we will cite the
following passage from an early Christian writer :—

"In the Eutychian Annals,[1] p. 37, it is stated that the
Eastern Christians say that when God ordered Noah to
build the Ark, He also directed him to make an instrument
of wood such as they make use of at this day (tenth century

---

[1] Eutychius was a Christian author of the sect of the Melchites. He was born
at Cairo in 876 A.D. His real name was Sayyid Batrak, but when chosen Patriarch
of Alexandria he took the name of Eutychius. The title of his book was *Annals
from the Beginning of the World to the Year* 900. An extract from the Annals of
the Church of Alexandria was published by Selden in Arabic and Latin in 1642,
and the whole book in Arabic and Latin by Pococke in 1659, with a Preface by
Selden.

A.D.) in the East, instead of bells, to call the people to church. It is named in the Arabic *Nûgûs*, and in the modern (tenth century) Greek *Sumandra*. On this he was to strike three times every day, not only to call together the workmen that were building the Ark, but to give him an opportunity of admonishing his people of the impending deluge, which would certainly destroy them if they did not repent."

It seems clear that the above quoted passage has reference to the use of a clapper such as those at present in use in Toledo. There is also not much room for doubt that the clapper had an Indian origin. A very similar instrument is to be found in India now : it is used in a most solemn part of Hindû worship. If one lives within ear-shot of a Hindû temple it may be heard every evening, being used in a service about sunset, which in many respects corresponds to the *Benediction* in Roman Catholic churches.

A sort of clashing sound may be heard soon after dusk, like that produced either by cymbals or a kind of clapper. The machine is on the same principle as those in Toledo; it has both a metallic and a wooden tone, owing to the small bits of metal attached to each spoke of the wheel. We had already frequently heard these sounds at a distance, but on one occasion only, when going over the palace at Ambêr, in the native State of Jaypur, curiosity impelled the writer to endeavour to witness what was then going on in the temple within that building, arriving just in time to see this machine at work, combined with the voices of the worshippers—a perfect Babel of discordant sounds was the result. A good view of the apparatus could be obtained over the heads of the natives, who were all prostrate on the ground, their foreheads on the pavement. As soon as the clashing noise ceased all rose.

On the ground immediately in front of a pedestal, on which was an idol, was a nine-wicked brass lamp of singular form ; this was then taken up and handed round to the members of the congregation, each one in turn passed his hands over the flames, and then bowing his head, seemed to repeat a prayer.

Though, as said above, modern Spanish customs are largely survivals of former Moorish ways, many of them appear to have a still more Eastern affinity. Thus, for example, the staple food of the Moors is, and has been for many generations, a preparation of wheat called *kûs-kûs*, consisting of flour rolled into tiny pellets, with a peculiar motion of the hand, and then boiled (or rather steamed), and served either with ungainly-looking lumps of boiled mutton or with various kinds of sauces, each in its separate sauce-boat : some savoury and some sweet, and some very peppery. *Kûs-kûs* is eaten with a spoon ; but the peasant of the province of Murcia, in the South of Spain, is a rice-grower and a rice eater, as are the natives of many parts of the plains of India. He is ignorant of the use of knife, fork, or spoon, and, moreover, eats his rice in the same way as the Indian does, by working it up into a ball with his right hand, and tossing this into his mouth with the peculiar motion adopted by the Indian. The above facts were related in 1884 by an officer of long service in India, who had just been making a walking tour through that province, frequently obtaining food and a night's lodging in peasants' houses— adding also that he found certain Indo-Persian Hindustani words in use in that part of the country, such as *bartan*, for a plate. Again, the position of the cow-stall in the houses of many villages in Spain is similar to that already described in the hill districts in India and elsewhere. In the remoter parts of the north of the Spanish Peninsula, which we visited many years ago—before there were any railways in that country, and when the particular district of which we speak had only a year or two previously been provided with a carriage road,—one actually entered a house by the cattle stalls, and had to pick one's way through among a number of cows and goats, with perhaps a few pigs thrown in. This made it no easy matter for a stranger to find the staircase, which led up to the living rooms of the family. These when entered were invariably spotlessly clean. To give other instances, we would note that the women of Hindûstan carry their young children on the hip ; one of the child's legs hangs before, the other behind, the mother. The same mode of carrying children is not uncommon in Spain : it is doubtful whether it exists elsewhere in Europe. Also, the movements executed by Spanish gipsy girls when dancing are precisely those of the hired dancing women of Algeria and of the plains of India.

In Valencia there is a curious church called La Patriarca, which no woman is permitted to enter unveiled. The name given to this building at once suggests that it may be a very old one. The ritual adopted there is said to be very different from that of the other Roman Catholic churches in that city. The writer visited it on several occasions, but was never fortunate enough to be present at an ordinary Mass, for each time only a service for the repose of the souls of the deceased relations or friends of those who assisted at it, was being performed.

To find the origin of this custom, one should also turn to Asia. The Hindûs are in the habit of celebrating the anniversaries of the death of their relations monthly, and afterwards yearly. All who can afford to go thither, can at Benares perform an act of pûjâ (or worship) once for all, with the object of purifying the souls of their ancestors.

In Spain, if a person loses either parent, he observes the anniversary of the decease as long as he lives ; if his child, or a brother or sister dies, this is done for a certain number of years ; for an uncle, seven years only. A few days previously notices are sent to the relations and friends that such a service will be held. All meet at the church, clad in mourning, at the appointed hour.

At Tarragona we find sculptures and symbols which remind us both of Asian and Northern European mythology as regards the hare, the frog, and the serpent.

The *hare* has long been everywhere connected with the phenomena of the sky, though one does not quite see on what grounds this rests. Thus, sailors are said to have an idea that the presence of a dead hare on board ship will bring bad weather. Again, the Freyja of Norse legends, the wife of Odin, the storm god, acquired in Saxony the title of Wald-minchen, or wood nymph, and hares were her attendants. The hare was also evidently in older times regarded as a prominent actor in the change of the seasons in Spain. In the East it was closely connected with the moon, from a fancied resemblance of its spots to those of the hare, which has possibly given rise to the following myth of Indian origin,[1] very popular amongst the modern Burmese. " All creatures

[1] For Hare legends, see De Gubernatis, *Zoological Mythology*, vol. ii., pp. 76-82.

were making offerings to the Buddha, who was engaged in preaching the Sacred Law. The hare bethought him that he too must give some alms. But what had he to give? Man might bring costly gifts, the lion found it easy to render the tender flesh of the fawn, birds of prey brought dainty morsels, fish could practice no less dainty signs of devotion, even the ant was able to drag along grains of sugar and aromatic leaves ; but the hare, what had he? He might gather the most tender succulent shoots from the forest glades, but they were useless even to form a couch for the Teacher. There was nothing but his own body, and that he freely offered. The Supreme Lord declined the sacrifice, but in remembrance of the pious intention, placed the figure of the hare in the Moon, and there it remains as a symbol of the Lord of Night to the present day."

The frog, too, has a place in Indian mythology.[1] At sunrise and at sunset, the sun near the water is likened to a frog. Out of this notion arose a Sanskrit story. Bhêki, the frog, was once a beautiful girl, and one day when sitting near a well she was seen by a king, who asked her to be his wife. She consented, on condition that he should never show her a drop of water. One day, being tired, she asked the king for water. He forgot his promise, brought water, and Bhêki disappeared—that is to say, the sun disappeared when it touched the water.

Lastly, it has already been shown in the earlier portion of this work that the serpent is intimately bound up with Indian mythology.[2] It may be a coincidence, but it is surely

[1] For Frog legends, see De Gubernatis, *Zoological Mythology*, vol. ii., pp. 71, 72.
[2] *Ibid.*, vol. ii., pp. 389-419.

a singular one, that these three animals—the hare, the frog, and the serpent—should all be found on one piece of sculpture in bas-relief at the base of a column in the south-west corner of the Cloisters of the Cathedral at Tarragona, *vide* Plate XXII, Fig 1. This building is said to date from the beginning of the twelfth century. It is not impossible that the original significance of these symbols was recognised by its designers as indicating the Storm, the Sun Snake (or perhaps the principle of evil), and the Sun itself; or, on the other hand, they may have been only forms handed down by tradition, and no meaning have been attached to them. Another capital of a pillar (Plate XXII, Fig. 3) in the same building has a frog in the centre. The animal is on its back with its limbs extended; two serpents, one on each side, appear to be attacking it.

The capital of yet another column in these Cloisters (see Plate XXII, Fig. 2) possesses a still more decided Eastern character. On the extreme left of Fig. 2 is a figure, half man, half horse,—the Centaur of Greek Mythology, and the European representative of the Gandharvas, Narads, Kinnaras or aerial beings of India, who were regarded as demi-gods. The Centaur, armed with a cross-bow, is aiming at a dragon, represented as an animal with a wide mouth, rolling eyes, and two short straight horns projecting from the forehead. The dragon, in short, belongs to a type which is familiar to all of us on articles coming from China. That Empire was in all probability the original home of this monster, for it seems still rampant there.

Lastly, to complete the Asiatic character of the Tarragona sculptures, on the extreme right is represented a man in the act of stabbing the dragon with a long spear. His dress is of a distinctly Central Asian or rather Persian type. There is yet another point of connection between Spain and the East, which should be noted before quitting this subject.

The inhabitants of the provinces on both sides of the Pyrenean frontier are Basques, and therefore one is not surprised to find that certain symbols and customs have found their way over the mountains from Spain into France, and have there survived, owing to the circumstance that the peculiar language spoken by the Basque people has isolated them a good deal from their neighbours. At St Jean-de-Luz, on the French side of the border, on the feast of St John the Baptist, who is the patron saint of that town, the people get up what are called *Pastorales* or representations in a versified narrative form. Their character varies—treating sometimes of secular, sometimes of religious subjects. The actors are invariably of the male sex ; where women's parts occur they are taken by young lads clad in female attire. The same play, if one may style it such, is carried on for some days, with intervals for rest and refreshment. Passion and secular plays are, however, very far from being confined to Spain or India. They seem to have been prevalent all over Europe and Asia for many centuries. The acting and the recital of the Râmâyana in India lasts several days in succession, and there also the female parts are taken by youths in women's dress. Certain other dances are also performed in Asia by men and boys, the latter dressed as women.

Among the Kahârs or palanquin-bearer caste in Northern India, dances in imitation of the *nâch* are commonly held, in which the women's parts are performed by youths dressed up as girls. There is a representation of such a dance on pottery in the Oxford Indian Institute.

Spain has taken some of its manners and customs from Persia, as well as from India. It is generally well known that should a stranger admire a Spaniard's house, or any of his possessions, his host in his most courteous manner will say : " Señor, you know that this house and all it contains is yours."

Sir William Ouseley, in the early part of the present century, relates in his *Travels in Persia and elsewhere*, his own experience when on his tour. On leaving Servistân, a large and populous village on his route between Shirâz, Tassa, and Darab, on which occasion he had been given the best room in a house, he was asked with much ceremony by his host, "how he had passed the night," adding : " I trust that thou hast enjoyed repose ; a person should sleep soundly in his own house ; does not this with all it contains belong to thee ? "

Pietro della Valle, a Sicilian, who travelled in Persia and elsewhere in the East between the years 1617 and 1626, in a series of letters to various friends, gives the following description of the method of warming an apartment—which he found both in Kurdistân and in Ispahan. He says :—
" They make fires in their rooms, but not with a chimney, but in a kind of oven in the ground, which they call *tennòr* (a word of Arabic origin). They make a hole about eight inches in depth (it may either be round or square), and in order that the fire may burn the quicker and easier, they place within this hollow space a vase of terra cotta made to fit it ; into this vessel they put live wood ashes, or they use charcoal

or other materials which speedily become alight. This done, they put over the place a wooden bench like a small low table ; over this they spread a coverlet, one of those which are thickly wadded, this reaches down to the ground, and extends over the floor on all sides. By thus keeping in the warmth of the fire, the effect of a stove is produced, and the whole apartment effectually heated. At meal times, or when engaged in conversation, some of these people also, when going to sleep, place themselves on rugs on the floor in a seated position—the shoulders resting on cushions placed against the wall.

" The *tennòr* is invariably in such a position that there is an equal distance between it and the walls of the room, on two sides at least. Only the hands and the rest of the body are beneath the coverlet, thus the whole person feels the effect of the penetrating and most agreeable warmth without the head being affected by it." " I can assure you," he continues, " I have never found any method of heating for the winter as pleasant as this, and I should wish to introduce it into Italy."

Apparently Pietro della Valle did carry this idea back with him to Europe. This system did, as it were, put its foot down in South Italy and in Sicily, where both high and low use the *brasèro* or brazier of hot embers in cold weather, since few of the rooms in the palazzi and the older houses possess either fireplaces or stoves ; but there the table and its coverlet have either disappeared, or they never found favour.

In Spain, however, the Persian system exists in its entirety. In Seville may still be seen in common use an almost similar apparatus to that described by Pietro della Valle.

The floors of the rooms being of wood, the arrangement is necessarily slightly different from the Persian one, but the principle is the same. The Spanish custom is to place in the centre of the room a round table from forty to fifty inches in diameter, the top is pierced with numerous round holes, each about the size of a shilling, thus leaving a free passage for the warm air coming up from the large copper vessel placed beneath, which is filled with live embers. This does not rest upon the floor, but fits into a wooden circle attached to the legs of the table at about twelve inches from the ground. The top of the table is covered with a large green cloth, which extends down to the floor and covers a large portion of it. This mode of heating would appear to be very generally practised in Seville, many such tables may be seen exposed for sale in the carpenters' shops in the town. Another Asiatic custom in the same connection seems also to have localised itself in one district only in Europe.

The natives of Kashmir are in the habit during the cold weather of carrying about a small pot covered with basket-work called a *kangri*; when in use it is filled with hot embers. On preparing to go to sleep these people very frequently put their kangri with its ignited contents inside the breast part of their upper garment, a practice which very often results in their being severely burnt about the chest, as it would seem they are very heavy sleepers.

The kangri appears to have found a home in one part of Italy only. In Florence, during the winters, which are very severe, no Florentine woman of the lower classes walks abroad without carrying her *Scaldino*, a reproduction of the kangri of Kashmir. Dr Hultzsch has shown that the use

of portable fireplaces or braziers was known in India—in
Kashmir—as early as the twelfth century A.D., and here we
have their use in Persia (and if Della Valle's word *tennòr* be
right, in Arabia also), as well as in Spain and Italy, in a
manner implying a long previous history.

There is a most remarkable collection of sculptures in the
Archæological Museum at Madrid; these, up to 1884 at least,
had puzzled the most learned antiquarians. They do not
seem to us to be so well known to the world in general as
they deserve, and as the Spanish Government was then said
to have bought a portion only of what was found, it is to be
hoped that some may still find their way into Art Museums
at South Kensington and elsewhere. The Madrid collection
consists of statues discovered in 1870-71 on a hill called *El
Cerro de los Angeles* near Yecla, a small village in the province of Murcia. In an article published in the *Athenæum*
of July 6th, 1872, Señor Juan Raño (author of the *South
Kensington Handbook on Spanish Art*) gives it as his opinion
" that they do not all belong to the same period." He holds
" that some are anterior, and that others are posterior, to the
Christian era," and adds, " in all of them there is a marked
Oriental influence. It is probable that the *Cerro de los
Angeles* was the seat of different civilisations, unless some of
these objects proceed from different localities."

In fact, on studying the various types of physiognomy and
of dress apparent in these statues, one is tempted to imagine
that they may in past ages have adorned the Museum of some
collector of antiquities who lived a thousand years ago. We
will here give a description of some of the most remarkable
ones. A nearly life-sized figure is a counterpart of the

Egyptian god Isis, while many of the heads bear a strong resemblance to certain statues found in 1884 on the island of Cyprus, of which the author has seen drawings. The greater number are female figures in a standing position, but there is one male life-sized figure, said to be that of a priest, and also a few detached male heads. Some of them are inscribed with Greek characters; others bear certain marks which at that time none of the learned had been able to decipher. One or two of the figures have the hair arranged in the Egyptian fashion; some have a veil arranged like the *Sârî* of the Hindû women; others again have the hair dressed very high and the veil put over it. These remind one of the Sikh women of the Panjâb; some again look like Lapp women. One or more large heads, presumably male ones, wear turbans; while a small male figure of Egyptian type has strands of hair brought down on each side of the face and twisted into a coil beneath the chin; but, strange to say, not one male figure is bearded, which would seem to point to a non-Aryan origin. A little male statue, about ten inches high, possesses in attitude and features the perfect look of repose peculiar to the statues of Buddha; the resemblance is still further carried out in the arrangement of the hair and of the folds of the robe.

The most interesting point in these sculptures as regards the subject of Symbolism is, that all the female figures carry pots in their hands at about the middle of the waist. From some of these vessels flames are issuing, which would seem to mark these figures as representing the votaries of some religion connected with the Sun or with Fire. One very remarkable female statue holds a pot of this kind, and on her breast are symbols of the Sun and Moon : a large Star is between them. On her robe also, just below the knees, is sculptured a serpent, a tree (?), and other apparently unfinished symbols, which are therefore not clearly distinguishable.

Who the people were that made these statues is a complete mystery : it seems hardly possible that they could have been the work of the same race of people.

Now that all my observations, discursive as they have been, have drawn to a close, let me say a few last words as to the lesson that such studies as these imply.

Doubtless many other points of resemblance between the manners and customs of Asia and Europe still remain to be enumerated, and if—*pace* the latest researches—we once open our eyes to the possibility that Asia was the cradle of most of the nations of Europe, a new light seems to break in upon us, and any symbols or customs which are common to both continents acquire for us a value which they had not before. They seem to assist us in tracing the rise and growth of religious feeling, of arts and manufactures, amongst European peoples of whose history and actions we are, and must otherwise remain, absolutely ignorant. We are compelled to own that the people of the so-called Bronze Age were not the Keltic savages we once imagined them to be ; that the people of the Stone Age were clever in their generation, and that the worshippers of the Sun and Moon who adored those planets because they thought that to them they owed the fertility of the soil, were the pioneers of civilisation.

We may learn a good deal in other ways too by studying what has been left us by these prehistoric races. It is evident that they put the best of their brain and hand work —their whole energy and knowledge—into whatever they executed.

Even with our modern perfect appliances, we can in some respects hardly equal, much less surpass, what they accomplished with the rudest tools.

FINIS.

" To see a world in a grain of sand,
    And a heav'n in a wild flower,
Hold infinity in the palm of your hand,
    And eternity in an hour."—WILLIAM BLAKE.

" A symbol is a sign included in the idea which it represents ; an actual part taken to represent the whole, or a lower form or species used as the representative of a higher of the same kind."—COLERIDGE.

" A myth is a narrative framed for the purpose of expressing some general truth. . . . A symbol is a silent myth, which impresses the truth which it conveys not by successive stages, but at once [*sun ballo*] throws together significant images of some truth."—WILLIAM FLEMING.

" The thoughts of all the greatest and wisest men have been expressed through mythology."—RUSKIN.

DATE DUE

NOV 3 0 1995		
FEB 0 7 1996		
APR 2 7 1998		
JUN 2 8 1999		
DEC 1 3 2002		

Demco, Inc. 38-293